USSR vs USA
THE **ABM** AND THE
CHANGED
STRATEGIC MILITARY BALANCE

USSR USA

AMERICANA
by ACROPOLIS

THE **ABM** AND THE CHANGED STRATEGIC MILITARY BALANCE

A study by a special American Security Council Committee of 31 experts,

Co-Chaired by:

DR. WILLARD F. LIBBY, *Nobel Laureate*
Director of Geophysics and Planetary Physics, U.C.L.A.

DR. WILLIAM J. THALER
Chairman, Physics Department, Georgetown University

GENERAL NATHAN F. TWINING, USAF (Ret.)
*Former Chief of Staff, USAF, and Chairman
Joint Chiefs of Staff*

PUBLISHED BY
Acropolis Books
WASHINGTON, D. C. 20009

in cooperation with American Security Council Press

Published by
ACROPOLIS BOOKS
*Colortone Building, 2400 17th St., N.W.
Washington, D.C. 20009*

FIRST PRINTING, MAY, 1969

SECOND EDITION, JUNE, 1969

Printed in the United States of America by
Colortone Creative Printing, *Washington, D.C. 20009*

Cover Design by Design and Art Studio 2400, Inc.

Library of Congress Catalog Number 76-92225
Standard Book Number 87491-400-0 (cloth)
87491-401-9 (paper)

TABLE OF CONTENTS

LIST OF FIGURES

Foreword

This study has been prepared at the request of the American Security Council, which asked us to make an assessment of the need for a missile defense based on *unclassified sources only*.

In order to properly consider the question of missile defense, we have also analyzed other aspects of the U.S.S.R. vs U.S.A. strategic military balance and the trends affecting that balance.

Sources

This study is based on analysis and evaluation of hundreds of unclassified sources published from May 1967 through April 1969. For the period prior to May 1967, we drew upon a previous ASC study on *The Changing Strategic Military Balance U.S.A. vs U.S.S.R.* which was published in June 1967 at the request of the House Armed Services Committee.

In this study we have used Department of Defense figures wherever available and consistent with other unclassified sources. The other unclassified sources against which DOD figures have been considered ranged from military, military-strategic, and scientific books, treatises, journals and limited distribution studies, trade and technical journals and magazines and publications of general and popular circulation, news magazines and newspapers.

We wish especially to acknowledge the benefits derived from the research efforts of the Aerospace Technology Division of the Library of Congress. This is the Nation's outstanding resource for behind-the-Iron Curtain publications.

Emphasis on Capabilities of Strategic Forces

This study focuses on strategic military forces. It does not report on other military and non-military conflict forces used by or available to each side. In this connection, it should be noted that until now the principal Soviet conflict thrust has been in the political warfare arena. For example, Communist efforts in "wars of national liberation" such as in South Viet Nam, subversive activities, and psychological warfare are not included in this study. Yet, from a strategic military balance point of view, Communist psychological warfare efforts aimed at reducing western military strength and readiness can be as important an influence on the balance as the U.S.S.R.'s build-up of strategic forces.

We have emphasized the trend in strategic military *capabilities* of the U.S.S.R. vs the U.S.A. This criterion is more important than one based upon *intentions* because one can easily be deceived by intentions but not as readily by capabilities.

If one finds an increasing *capability* for warfare on the part of a self-declared enemy, it is only common sense and prudence to prepare an adequate defense. This judgment is reinforced if one finds that the enemy's stated objectives and goals parallel his increasing capabilities.

For this reason, we have also carefully examined the stated objectives and military doctrine of the Soviet Union.

Intelligence Lag

In the development of military capabilities, the Soviets continue to have an inherent advantage. Even with the most advanced intelligence detection techniques, we do not know nearly as much about them as they know about us. Our society is an open one and our planned future weapons systems are debated and announced in advance.

The Soviets, on the other hand, conceal their new weapons systems from us until testing or deployment actually takes place. Even then doubt usually remains concerning the exact capability and ultimate quantitative level of each new weapons system.

Public Need to Know

The practice in the Department of Defense and the intelligence community has been to classify information about the U.S.S.R.'s capabilities and intentions even though the Soviets know that the U.S.A. has the information. Official secrecy concerning our knowledge of Soviet capabilities is supposed to be justified by the need to keep information from potential enemies. There are areas where secrecy is necessary. Unfortunately, however, we have carried secrecy to the point of obsession and this obsession has frequently been far more successful in keeping vital information from the American people, from Congress, and from our allies, than it has been in keeping it from the Soviets.

But perhaps the gravest consequence of excessive secrecy is that it undermines the democratic system because democracy simply will not work if the people do not have the essential facts. This is dramatically demonstrated by the current debate on the ABM because there is no question that the Administration has been handicapped by public ignorance of some of the vital facts about the growth of Soviet strategic forces.

Secretary of Defense Melvin Laird is making a start toward bringing the klieg light of truth to bear on our actual national security situation. This change in policy has its handicaps because some of the hard truths contradict the "all is well" impression given by his predecessors. Some may argue that the frank and forthright testimony of Secretary Laird, Deputy Secretary of Defense Packard and Chairman of the Joint Chiefs of Staff General Wheeler showed up some of the critical weaknesses of our defense posture and revealed some heretofore classified intelligence information. *But the strength of America and its free institutions has always resided in the public's understanding of the issues and problems that confront our representative government.*

In a campaign speech in September of 1960, the late John F. Kennedy declared:

> "Some people say it is wrong to say that we could be stronger; that it's dangerous to say that we could be more secure. But in times such as this, I say it is wrong and dangerous for any American to keep silent about our future if he is not satisfied with what is being done to preserve that future."

It is our sincere hope that this study will be useful to those Americans who are seeking more facts in order to better understand current national security issues and problems.

Respectfully submitted,

Signed/ Dr. Willard F. Libby, Co-chairman
Dr. William J. Thaler, Co-chairman
General Nathan F. Twining, Co-chairman

General Paul D. Adams, USA (Ret.)
Dr. Harold M. Agnew
Professor James D. Atkinson
Duncan Bauman
Peter Bruce Clark
Admiral Robert L. Dennison USN (Ret.)
Ambassador Elbridge Durbrow (Ret.)
Admiral H. D. Felt, USN (Ret.)
Robert W. Galvin
Vice Admiral Elton W. Grenfell, USN (Ret.)
Dr. Montgomery Johnson
Vice Admiral Fitzhugh Lee, USN (Ret.)
Vice Admiral R. E. Libby, USN (Ret.)
Dr. Nicholas Nyaradi
Professor Stefan T. Possony

General Thomas S. Power, USAF (Ret.)
Brig. General Robert C. Richardson, USAF (Ret.)
Ira G. Ross
Vice Admiral W. A. Schoech, USN (Ret.)
General Bernard A. Schriever, USAF (Ret.)
Lewis L. Strauss
Dr. Kenneth Street, Jr.
Dr. A. D. Suttle
Dr. Edward Teller
Rear Admiral Chester C. Ward, USN (Ret.)
Dr. Kenneth Watson
General Albert C. Wedemeyer, USA (Ret.)
Dr. Eugene P. Wigner

As special subcommittee of the
National Strategy Committee of the
American Security Council.

Summary

The Soviet Union has jumped into the lead in overall strategic missile strength by making optimum use of a much smaller economic base than the United States and is operating on a war economy basis. Therefore, an American ABM system is the soundest insurance for peace and against war that the United States can buy in 1969, for the 1970's.

Far from being an offensive weapon, the ABM is in reality insurance against war. It may well be, in fact, the single most important step the United States can take toward a real and lasting peace at this moment in history.

The study concludes that it is no longer necessary to suppose . . . that the Soviets *will* aim for strategic military superiority. Reality now conforms to theory. We now *know* that the Soviet's military objective is strategic superiority because they have passed "parity" and are still building.

The combined total of ICBMs, IR/MRBMs (Intermediate and Medium Range Missiles) and SLMs (Sea-Launched Missiles) is now estimated as 2,750 for the U.S.S.R. to 1,710 for the U.S.A.

Evidence of the near "war economy" which the Soviet Union maintains, the subcommittee pointed out, is provided by the fact that:

. . . The overall military budget of the U.S.S.R. is already essentially equal to or greater than the U.S. budget, especially when costs peculiar to Vietnam are excluded from the U.S. figures . . .

Although the gross national product of the United States runs almost twice that of the gross in the U.S.S.R., the U.S.S.R. is investing two to three times more in strategic military forces annually . . .

The U.S.S.R. may invest at least $50 to $100 billion more in strategic forces between now and 1975, than the United States, unless the relative trends change substantially.

As a consequence of this greater effort, not only has the military power of the Soviet Union grown more rapidly than that of the U.S.A., but it has rapidly overtaken the forces of the United States in new concepts and new weapons systems.

The U.S.S.R. now has whole families of military (and naval) weapons systems that the United States does not have in its inventory.

The U.S.S.R. has adopted what the subcommittee described as "innovative policies" to take advantage of both offensive and defensive opportunities.

For example—the Soviets:

—presently enjoy a clear lead in space orbital weapons . . . properly deployed, a significant number, let us say 100, could be in a position to attack the United States in a matter of seconds after the button was pushed in the Kremlin . . .

—have an estimated 1,000 Intermediate and Medium Range Missiles which are primarily aimed at Europe and now completely pin Europe down . . .

—have very large—50-100 megaton nuclear weapons which were tested in 1961-62 . . . adapted for missile delivery.

—have the Bear Bomber. It is the world's longest range, highest endurance bomber . . . an effective anti-shipping and anti-submarine attack aircraft with air-to-surface attack missiles on board.

Furthermore, the Soviet Union has been developing a sophisticated ABM defense system for ten years and now has anti-ballistic missiles deployed around Moscow and in a "Blue Belt" defense line described by Marshal Malinovsky as being "for the defense of the entire territory of the Soviet Union."

In connection with their missile defense program, the Soviets are developing a comprehensive civil defense program . . . spending about ten times as much effort as is the United States in providing the Soviet society an adequate civil defense. Moreover, civil defense in the Soviet Union is related directly to overall Soviet military strategy.

These findings become most significant when considered against the background of announced Soviet objectives and the continuing assertions of Soviet leaders that they are preparing for any eventuality that might trigger a nuclear war in their determination to achieve long-stated Communist goals, worldwide.

In both word and deed, the Soviets have shown that they regard the world struggle as a fight to the finish between two diametrically opposed social systems. Moreover, it is a fight the Soviets intend to win.

In the face of this Soviet drive for strategic superiority, coupled with announced Communist aims and the near "war economy" atmosphere prevailing in the Soviet Union, the special subcommittee agreed that the United States must create a missile defense system to protect our nuclear deterrent.

An ABM system is not a cure-all for the security of the United States ... but (it) is an essential component in the network of military systems designed to give the American people a seamless garment of security in an age of acute danger.

On March 14, 1969, President Nixon announced that his Administration planned to modify the Sentinel missile defense system approved by Congress under the Johnson Administration by using it first to defend some U.S. retaliatory missiles rather than to defend cities. This modification was named the "Safeguard" system ...

Safeguard is a modest, limited proposal. It is subject to constant review, as conditions change.

Nevertheless, the Safeguard ABM has become the focus of a major national debate. It has become a symbolic issue with many. Some of those who oppose the emphasis given to national defense expenditures have clearly chosen Safeguard as the issue on which to join in opposition.

The Safeguard debate has thus assumed such importance that all major defense decisions in the future will very likely be prejudiced if Safeguard is rejected.

In conclusion:

ABM is a method of deterrence which will save lives and not destroy them.

It is more consistent with the moral objectives of the United States for this country to provide more effective ways of protecting people than to base our deterrent power wholly upon our ability to kill people in other countries or "accept" heavy casualties at home.

On balance, Safeguard makes sense:
  . . it makes sense to defend our retaliatory missile sites;
  . . it makes sense to defend our air bases;
  . . it makes sense to defend our national command centers in the nation's capital;
  . . it makes sense because the cost is relatively low and the program is subject to yearly review;
  . . it makes sense to defend against the Chinese threat of the mid-70s;
  . . it makes sense because we are not foreclosing the future.

We are leaving our options open.

CHAPTER I

U.S.S.R. VERSUS U.S.A. OBJECTIVES

Contrast Between Political Objectives

"Ever harder times lie ahead for capitalism. The fact that it is doomed is becoming increasingly clear. But the capitalists will never surrender their rule voluntarily. The working class and the laboring masses will achieve victory only in the course of stubborn class battles . . . At our Congress today we once more repeat the appeal: close ranks more solidly for the struggle against the common enemy!"

> Leonid I. Brezhnev, First Secretary Communist Party of the Soviet Union March 29, 1966 report to the 23rd Congress of the Communist Party of the Soviet Union

"Yet our basic goal remains the same, a peaceful world community of free and independent states—free to choose their own future and their own system, so long as it does not threaten the freedom of others."

> John F. Kennedy, State of the Union Message, January 11, 1962

"The Soviet Union is a power which is still attempting to expand around the world. The United States, on the other hand, is a power whose goal is only peace. We are not attempting to dominate any part of the world; we are merely trying to assure the right of freedom of choice for other nations."

> Richard M. Nixon, *Nixon on the Issues,* October 17, 1968, p. 17

The most important difference between the political objectives of the United States versus the Soviet Union is that the Soviets aim to win the world by imposing their system on everyone else, whereas the United States does not.

Because of this difference, the Soviet Union's political objectives clearly extend beyond protecting its own national security or its own national interests, even though these are, of course, vital components of its objectives.

In both word and deed, the Soviets have shown that they regard the world struggle as a fight to the finish between two diametrically opposed social systems. Moreover, it is a fight the Soviets intend to win. As *Military Strategy* puts it:

> "The program of the CPSU states that the present era, the fundamental makeup of which is transition from capitalism to socialism, is an era of conflict between two opposite social systems, an era of the downfall of capitalism and the liquidation of the colonial system, the era of the transition of more

and more nations to socialism, of the triumph of socialism and communism on a world-wide scale." [1]

This distinction between the goals of the United States and the Soviet Union is utterly crucial. In the pursuit of its objective the United States has no reason to attack the Soviet Union. We have never shown any interest in attacking the Soviets. The Soviet Union has, on the other hand, a definite motivation to overthrow or attack the United States because we are the principal national embodiment of the social system—capitalism—which the Soviets have sworn to eliminate. We alone have the strength to stand between them and their objective of world domination.

This is the reality of the situation. Not only do we have no *objective* which requires our initiating an attack against the Soviet Union, but we have carefully tailored our nuclear arsenal to exclude all weapons *designed* to initiate such an attack, or with which we could even credibly threaten such an attack. We have no hundreds of missiles with 25 megaton warheads. We have no orbital or fractional orbital nuclear bombardment systems whose utility is solely to deprive defensive forces of sufficient warning time to survive a surprise attack. We have neither the *capability* nor the *intent* of initiating nuclear war against the Soviets.

But the picture the Soviets seek to present to the world, to their own people, and even to the more naive among our people, is the exact reverse of reality. The West, led by the United States, they charge, is planning and preparing war against the Socialist countries, primarily against the Soviet Union. This has been the official Kremlin line since Stalin first promoted it in the period of 1948-52. Khrushchev reasserted it in his January 6, 1961 speech.

The Soviets have consistently contended that the West, led by the United States, was preparing to launch a nuclear war against the Soviet Union and that they could and would "prevent" the launching of such a war. They have contended that capitalism has been "doomed" by history, "but will never surrender voluntarily." The Communist Summit said it in 1960, Khrushchev echoed it in 1961, and it has now been repeated again as recently as April 21, 1969, by Gen. Alexei Yepishev, head of the Political Administration of the Soviet Defense Ministry. Writing in *Kommunist*, official journal of the Soviet Communist Party Central Committee (thus indicating the

---

1. *Military Strategy,* Marshal V. D. Sokolovsky, editor, Moscow, 1968, Third Russian edition. The major work on Soviet military strategy approved by the Communist Party of the Soviet Union.

highest official sanction)[2] Yepishev declared that Western "imperialists are hypocritically preparing for a new world war", and warned that "a third world war, if imperialism is allowed to start one, would be the decisive class conflict between two antagonistic social systems," and that it would "guarantee the construction of socialism and communism."

This part of the declaration is significant—not because it is unprecedented, but because it repeats almost word for word the charges made in Khrushchev's speech of January 6, 1961, and constitutes evidence that the Soviets have never departed from the strategic doctrine set out in that speech.

Yepishev went on to say;

(1) Western attempts to brand nuclear war as unacceptable were aimed:

> "to confuse the popular masses concerning the class political character, the true purpose of a possible war";

(2) And he cited "the classical Leninist teaching" which holds that "a series of frightful clashes"

between Communism and the West is inevitable, still applies in the nuclear age; and

(3) If the new war should be initiated by the imperialist states, "this war would be a continuation of the criminal, reactionary aggressive policies of imperialism",

but that

> "from the side of the Soviet Union . . . it would be the continuation of the revolutionary policies of freedom and independence of the Socialist state, *a legal and justified counteraction to aggression.*" (emphasis added)

The following excerpt from a March 19, 1969 article in the official newspaper of the Soviet Armed Forces, *Red Star* by Major General V. Reznichkenko gives further insight into Soviet military thinking. In an article significantly titled "The Art of Winning," General Reznichkenko states that

> "with the appearance and introduction of nuclear weapons into the armed forces a new stage began in the development of the theory of the military art. During the last 10 to 15 years our country has made a gigantic leap forward in its development. The armed forces have changed completely; thanks to the wise guidance of the CPSU and its Central Committee and the successes of Soviet economics, science and technology, our

---

2. as quoted in the *Washington Post*, April 27, 1969, p. 1.

armed forces have been equipped with the necessary number of various kinds of nuclear weapons with first class delivery systems, and also with new kinds of weapons and equipment."

And then General Reznichkenko raises the question of the use of surprise attack in war:

> "Surprise is a very important principle of military art which determines whether victory is achieved during combat actions. *Surprise makes it possible to anticipate the enemy in delivery strikes, takes him unawares,* paralyzes his will, sharply reduces his combat capability, disorganizes control, and creates favorable conditions for the defeat of even superior forces." (Emphasis added)

Thus it is cardinal to Soviet doctrine that the United States will be the losing side in the competition with Communism. And the losing side, they reason, will surely attempt to employ nuclear weapons in order to avert final defeat.

Khrushchev said it this way, in explaining why an agreement banning the use of nuclear weapons in war would not be effective:

> "The trouble is the losing side will always use nuclear weapons in the last resort to avoid defeat. If a man thinks he is going to die, he will take any steps." (Quoted in interview with English journalist Lord Thompson AP dispatch dtd. London, Aug. 15, 1964)

Thus by reversing reality to attribute to the United States an intention to use nuclear weapons in a desperation attempt to avert final defeat, the Soviets are able to merge their political objective of worldwide victory of their social system, with a high-sounding objective of averting a "nuclear world war." To them a "nuclear war" is a bilateral contest, involving a nuclear exchange. It should be no comfort to us, therefore, to dwell on their repeated statements that nuclear war is "not inevitable" or necessary to the victory of their system. That is an Aesopian way of saying they consider they have the capability of disarming us so effectively that we can neither launch nor wage a nuclear war.

Consequently, as President Nixon pointed out in his address to the NATO Ministers on April 10, 1969, our problem with the Soviet Union is far more than just a failure of communications.

Systemic Conflict

The Soviet theory of Systemic Conflict, which was used to justify the invasion of Czechoslovakia, makes it doubly clear why this is so. Their world view postulates inevitable class conflict between the "progressive" forces of revolution on the one hand and the "reactionary" forces of "imperialism" and "counterrevolution" on the other. This adds up to "the *decisive fact of our time . . . which is . . . the struggle between two opposing social systems—capitalism and socialism.*" (*Pravda*, September 25, 1968). Because Czechoslovakia was allegedly threatened by "counterrevolution," the "Commonwealth of Socialist Countries," led by the Soviet Union, had both the right and the obligation to intervene. This is the so-called "Brezhnev Doctrine." It was defined as follows by the chief of the Soviet Communist Party:

> "Military assistance, designed to avoid the threat to the socialist system . . . may be taken when the enemies of socialism within or without a country threaten the common interests of the socialist camp." (Speech to the Polish Party Congress, November 12, 1968)

The Czech invasion could be regarded primarily as a defensive *intra-system* operation made necessary because the forces of "imperialist capitalism" had made dangerous inroads into Czechoslovakia and had to be eradicated. But this defensive move could just as easily be turned into an offensive operation in the *inter-system* conflict. One need only recall the Kremlin's continuing campaign of threats and intimidation against West Germany to see how crucial this point is. The Czech invasion had the incidental effect of adding to the Soviet military threat to West Germany and to all of Western Europe.

The structure of systemic conflict is based upon the philosophy of man and history as it was developed by Marx and Engels and sharpened into operational principles by Lenin. This combination is called Marxism-Leninism. It postulates five historical socio-economic stages: primitive-communal, slave-owning, feudal, capitalist, and socialist/communist. It is the view of the Communists that their task is to serve as the "locomotive of history," in order to facilitate the transition, as rapidly as possible, of all world societies into the "utopian" fifth society, the communist society.

In such a situation there can be "peace", defined as "peaceful coexistence between states with opposite social systems", but there can never be an absence of conflict *per se*. This idea has been rejected again and again by Soviet spokesmen and is not a negotiable question, in the Soviet view.

Strategic military power is directly related to the Soviet political objective of the victory of their social system. This victory is to be achieved through the interplay of revolutionary disruption of opposing societies from within and overwhelming power politics by the Soviet Union from without. These together make up the two essential thrusts behind which the Soviets wage systemic conflict. Their expectation is that there will be a progressive, snowballing breakdown of the non-communist world as non-communist and especially U.S. society increasingly comes to lack both the will and the means to emerge successfully from Soviet-inspired or supported crisis situations. Soviet military power will likely support Soviet political objectives by 1) deterring U.S. military reactions to Communist politico-military moves and 2) achieving the final victory of the Communist system through threatened or actual nuclear attack on the United States.

It should be noted that the perennial argument about whether Soviet policy is primarily motivated by Russian imperialism or Communist ideology is essentially irrelevant under present circumstances. Whether the Soviet Union wishes world communism for its own sake or to satisfy the imperial ambitions of the U.S.S.R. is a question to which even the Soviet leadership might not be able to give an honest answer. What is a fact is that if the world Communist system finally prevails, it will do so when the power of the United States has been effectively destroyed or neutralized. The U.S.S.R. will then be in a military position to make its will prevail in any part of the world and the episode of Czechoslovakia and the "Brezhnev Doctrine" suggest that it will not be bashful in doing so.

Contrast Between U.S.-U.S.S.R. Strategic Objectives

a. Soviet strategic objectives.

It is understandable and logical that the Soviet political objective of systemic victory *requires*, almost by definition, absolute strategic superiority. From their point of view, a desperation U.S. first strike against the Soviet Union—in preference to systemic defeat—is a constant possibility. The Soviets must, therefore, be in a position to pre-empt this possibility by a first strike of their own. The general Soviet strategic objective is best summarized in the following excerpts from *Military Strategy* (Third edition, 1968):

> "Possibilities of averting surprise attack are constantly growing. Present means of reconnaissance detection and surveillance can opportunely disclose a significant portion of the measures of direct preparation of a nuclear attack by the enemy and in the very first minutes locate the mass launch of missiles and the take-off of aircraft belonging to the aggressor and, at the right time, warn the political leadership of the country about the impending danger. Thus, possibilities exist not to allow a surprise attack by an aggressor; to deliver nuclear strikes on him at the right time."

> "In its political and social essence, a new world war will be a decisive armed clash between two opposed world social

systems. This war will naturally end in victory for the progressive Communist social-economic system over the reactionary capitalist socio-economic system which is historically doomed to destruction. The guarantee for such an outcome of the war is the real balance between the political, economic, and military forces of the two systems, which has changed in favor of the socialist camp. However, victory in a future war will not come by itself. It must be thoroughly prepared for and assured."

The capability to pre-empt a suspected attack by the foe is also the capability to attack at leisure or to *threaten such an attack*.

It is no longer necessary to suppose from the foregoing that the Soviets *will* aim for strategic military superiority. Reality now conforms to theory. We now *know* that the Soviet's military objective is strategic superiority because they have passed "parity" (as will be indicated) and are still building.

United States Strategic Objectives

In line with its own political objectives of peace and world order, the United States is not arming to fight an aggressive war and wants only to defend itself and its allies. In his January 15, 1969 Posture Statement, former Secretary of Defense Clark M. Clifford summarized the basic U.S. strategy of deterrence as follows:

". . . we must be prepared to maintain at all times strategic forces of such size and character, and exhibit so unquestionable a will to use them in retaliation if needed, that no nation could ever conceivably deem it to its advantage to launch a deliberate nuclear attack on the United States or its allies. "While the general policy objective of deterrence has been clearly defined and firmly established in recent years, the size and character of the forces required for its support remain the subject of continuing debate."

The decision to build the Safeguard ABM system is now part of this "continuing debate." The U.S. strategic military objective *was* deterrence of war through building and deploying a massive nuclear strike capability. But this objective was limited by the past administration to what is known as "assured destruction," defined as the ability to inflict unacceptable losses on an attacker after conceding him the first blow. The U.S. doctrine now does not include the mission of neutralizing the enemy's striking forces (the "counterforce" concept).

In contrast, as we have shown above, the Soviets are building and deploying strategic forces to provide a capability of successful counterforce. This is the most important difference between the U.S. and U.S.S.R. military doctrine and strategic force objectives. This contrast is especially significant as we note that the Soviet Union is building and deploying an ABM system (counterforce) to neutralize U.S. ICBMs. The United States is not. This fundamental difference in strategy will aggravate the growing imbalance unless the people of the United States support the President in his decision to provide America with a missile defense force.

CHAPTER II

*INVESTMENTS IN STRATEGIC MILITARY
STRENGTH: A COMPARISON—U.S.S.R. VS. U.S.A.*

In first considering strategic military capabilities, a fundamental task is an appraisal of what the U.S.S.R. and U.S.A. are spending for military hardware services, research, and for developing and deploying strategic military systems.

Here we will consider the evidence of what the Soviet Union is doing—and has been doing for some time—in comparison to the U.S. effort despite the far less developed industrial base and economy of the U.S.S.R.

Overall Budget Comparison

Although the gross national product of the United States runs almost twice that of the gross in the U.S.S.R., the U.S.S.R. is investing 2-3 times more in strategic military forces annually. Comparisons (see Figures 1, 1a, 1b) for 1968 are (in billions):

	U.S.A.	U.S.S.R.
GNP	$820.0	$430.
Overall Defense	75.0	55.-70.
Strategic Forces	6.8	16.-17.3
Military R&D and Space	15.5	13.-17.0

No official figures are available on Soviet strategic forces investment. The American Security Council estimated in 1967 that the U.S.S.R. strategic military budget for 1967 was about 14.7 billion dollars. We used roughly the same percentage for 1969 and 1970. The range of uncertainty, we believe, from reviewing all sources, is about 15-20%. Mr. Laird said that "the Soviet Union, as far as offensive strategic weapons systems, is outspending the U.S. in the ratio of 3 to 2 converted to dollars." [3] We used Mr. McNamara's Posture Statement of 1968 where he gave the ratio of U.S. offensive to defensive forces of 3/1 and derived a figure of 16 billion dollars expended by the U.S.S.R. for strategic forces in 1968. Similarly, we calculated the Soviet 1969 figure to be 16-18 billion dollars. Figure 1b shows our plot of this data. U.S. expenditures lag obligation authority by about 2 years.

The U.S. News and World Report (Feb. 6, 1967, p. 34) estimated, as a result of their study, that almost 70 percent of the U.S.S.R. military budget was being devoted to strategic forces. Dr. Timothy Sosnovy estimated in 1964 that 30-40 percent of the Soviet military expendi-

---

3. Sec. Laird's press conference, Feb. 18, 1969, and his comments before Face the Nation, February 9, 1969.

tures (which run roughly twice the overt budget figure) were strategic forces. At that time, Dr. Sosnovy's careful analysis points out that this expenditure covered reserves for food and medicine as well as strategic forces.[4]

However, the rate of change, U.S./U.S.S.R. from '66 to '70 is most interesting. The U.S.S.R. may invest at least $50 to $100 billion more in strategic forces between now and 1975 than the United States, unless the relative trends change substantially.

In addition, the Soviets are investing heavily in military RDT&E in order to continue to develop modern new military weapons systems. As Figure 1c indicates, the Soviet military RDT&E expenditures for 1970 may be about $15-$20 billion compared with about $15 billion in the United States. (This assumes that U.S. military and space R&D is about 85% of the total Federal outlay.)

Even this figure may be conservative in view of the vigorous Soviet space program, nuclear weapons, the ICBMs, the IR/MRBMs, the ABMs, the nuclear submarines, the huge radars, civil defense and similar activities that are apparent throughout the Soviet Union. This is to say that the upper range of uncertainty shown in Figure 1c may be the more likely level of U.S.S.R. expenditures.

As a matter of some interest, Mr. J. P. Kozlowski of the National Science Foundation points out that the U.S.S.R. passed the U.S. in R&D investments in 1968 and may stay ahead of the U.S. in subsequent years. ($25.8 billion vs. $25.0 billion in 1968.)[5]

It is difficult to render in precise terms the scope of the Soviet strategic military effort, which embraces everything from space-warfare weapons to civil defense. But we can extrapolate from past Soviet accomplishments and activity in order to obtain an idea of the magnitude of the Soviet effort in comparison with the U.S. effort.

There are many other qualifying statements necessary to a full discussion of Figures 1, 1a, 1b, and 1c. Adjustments are necessary due to inflation. The large portion of the U.S. military budget diverted to the war in Viet Nam probably should be discounted somewhat in comparing the United States with the U.S.S.R. However, it is apparent that the United States is financing a war, whereas the U.S.S.R. is not (except for the provision of equipment). Yet, in spite of this, the military budget of the U.S.S.R. is already essentially equal to or considerably greater than the U.S. budget, especially when costs peculiar to Vietnam are excluded from the U.S. figures in 1969 and 1970.

---

4. Sosnovy, T., "The Soviet Military Budget," *Foreign Affairs*, April 1964, page 490 and discussions with the author.
5. J. P. Kozlowski, "R&D in the U.S.S.R.", *Science and Technology*, March 1969, p. 10.

COMPARISON OF MILITARY EXPENDITURES

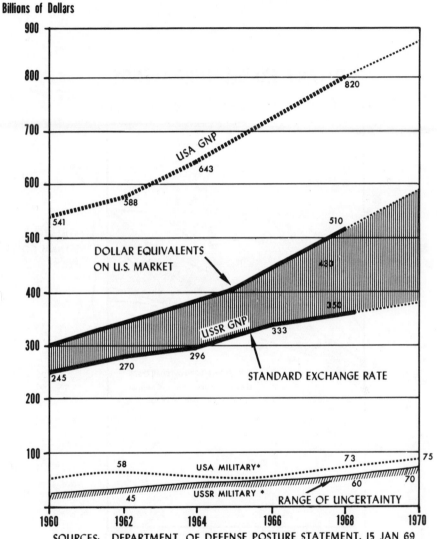

Billions of Dollars

USA GNP
820
643
588
541

DOLLAR EQUIVALENTS
ON U.S. MARKET
510
430

USSR GNP
350
333
296
270
245

STANDARD EXCHANGE RATE

73   75
58   USA MILITARY*
60   70
USSR MILITARY *   RANGE OF UNCERTAINTY
45

1960   1962   1964   1966   1968   1970

SOURCES: DEPARTMENT OF DEFENSE POSTURE STATEMENT, 15 JAN 69
           LIBRARY OF CONGRESS STUDIES (SOSNOVY)
           STANFORD RESEARCH INSTITUTE STUDIES (LEE)
           (SEE TEXT FOR DETAIL)
           * SEE FIGURE 1a FOR DETAILED COMPARISON
           (USSR FIGURES ARE MEAN OF FIGURE 1a)

Figure 1

MILITARY EXPENDITURE TRENDS

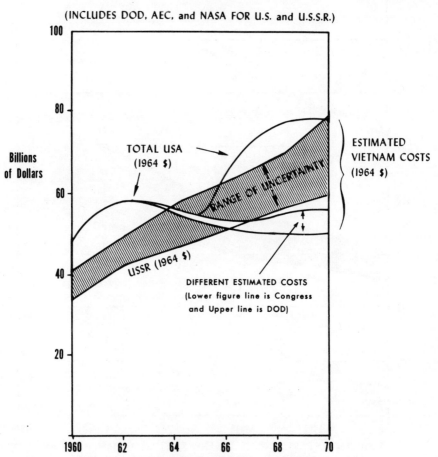

(INCLUDES DOD, AEC, and NASA FOR U.S. and U.S.S.R.)

Billions of Dollars

TOTAL USA (1964 $)

ESTIMATED VIETNAM COSTS (1964 $)

RANGE OF UNCERTAINTY

USSR (1964 $)

DIFFERENT ESTIMATED COSTS
(Lower figure line is Congress
and Upper line is DOD)

SOURCES: DEPARTMENT OF DEFENSE POSTURE STATEMENT, 15 JAN 69
LIBRARY OF CONGRESS STUDIES (SOSNOVY)
STANFORD RESEARCH INSTITUTE STUDIES (LEE)
(SEE TEXT FOR DETAIL)

Figure 1a

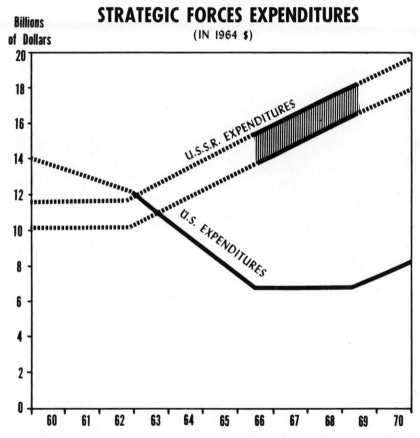

STRATEGIC FORCES EXPENDITURES
(IN 1964 $)

Billions
of Dollars

U.S.S.R. EXPENDITURES

U.S. EXPENDITURES

60   61   62   63   64   65   66   67   68   69   70

SOURCES: DEPARTMENT OF DEFENSE RELEASES, 15 JAN 69, 4 FEB 69, 18 FEB 69
LIBRARY OF CONGRESS STUDIES (SOSNOVY)
ASC STUDY, CHANGING STRATEGIC MILITARY BALANCE, USA/USSR,
1967, PAGE 23.   (SEE TEXT FOR DETAIL)

Figure 1b

RESEARCH, DEVELOPMENT, TECHNOLOGY and ENGINEERING EXPENDITURES

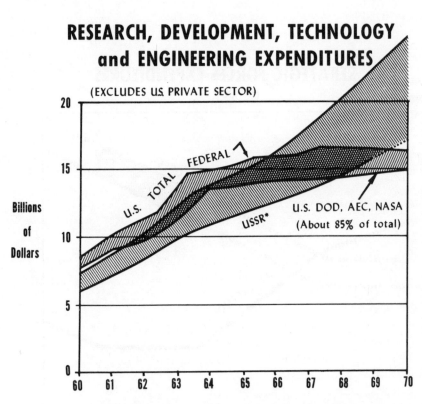

SOURCES: DEPARTMENT OF DEFENSE POSTURE STATEMENT, 15 JAN 69
LIBRARY OF CONGRESS STUDIES (SOSNOVY)
STANFORD RESEARCH INSTITUTE STUDIES (LEE)

KOZLOWSKI, J.P., SCIENCE AND TECHNOLOGY, 7 MARCH 1969,
"R&D IN THE USSR", PAGE 10.
(SEE TEXT FOR DETAIL)

* SEE FIGURE 1a FOR DETAILED COMPARISON (WE HAVE ASSUMED MILITARY
TO BE ABOUT 75-85% TOTAL)

Figure 1c

The data presented in Figures 1-1c have been compiled partly from Aerospace Technology Division studies at the Library of Congress with the expert help of Dr. Sosnovy who has just completed a review of Soviet investments for military and military research and development (see also Figure 2). We have also used Stanford Research Institute studies in making our overall judgments. We are especially indebted to Richard B. Foster of the Stanford Research Institute and .members of his staff, especially William Lee for permitting us to use some of the results of his research which, among other things, indicates ranges of uncertainty in the data.

Of course the validity of even a GNP figure for the U.S.S.R. is subject to question and interpretation, but in spite of all these difficulties with economic and budgetary figures, we believe even general comparisons are useful as guides to understanding and decision.

One overall observation from our study of Soviet investments should be made.

Over 40 years ago, the Soviet Defense Commissar, M. Frunze, wrote: "In any new undertaking, economic, cultural, or other . . . one must always ask the question: What relation does this undertaking have to the task of protecting the nation? Is there any possibility of letting it serve specific military purposes also without impairing peaceful goals?" (A. N. Lagorskiy "Strategy and Economics", Moscow, 1957, page 194, quoted in Sosnovy, 1964.) This general principle still holds throughout the Soviet economy.

It is true there are strains in the Soviet economy, inefficiencies, gaps, and downright wasted resources. But does this mean fewer revenues go to the military forces?

"Long before Goebbels, the people of the Soviet Union truly knew the meaning of 'guns before butter' . . . . in 1934 direct military expenditures rose from 1,655 million rubles to 5,000 million rubles, or more than trebled. The increases of 1961, 1962, and 1963 showed that the Soviet Government is as able under Khrushchev as under Stalin to increase military expenditures to any level desired." (Sosnovy, 1964, page 494)

The evidence points to the continuation of this trend of concentration on military production. The two basic goals of the 8th 5-year plan (1966-1970) were announced to be:

"to strengthen the defensive might of the country,"
and to provide
"a substantial rise in the standard of living of the people." [6]

---

6. *Pravda*, Feb. 20, 1966, page 1.

But overall Soviet economic investment policy has been historically and is now "that guns come before butter." [7]

Central Command and Control

The Soviets also have the advantage, at least in the development of conflict doctrine and the means to wage conflict that comes from their overall control structure—that is to say, the U.S.S.R. proceeds with whatever military systems it deems essential and does not have to reckon (as much as U.S. leadership does) with the force of inadequate public understanding or opposition from those who do not agree with the country's goals. The United States, which rightfully takes pride in its democratic system of decision-making has to overcome sincere doubters and deliberate obstructionists through a lengthy process of public education and analysis of the issues and problems involved. No American would willingly surrender his country's system of free inquiry and open discussion, but it has to be recognized that a totalitarian regime is able to plan to develop and to deploy weapon systems more rapidly because of this centralized character of decision-making.

The high priority given to military requirements in the Soviet Union is a matter of historical record. However, the priority since 1965 is especially noteworthy.

The Central Committee of the Communist Party, of course, runs the U.S.S.R. Of the 360 members, 36 are active duty flag rank officers. Most are 4 or 5 star admirals, generals, or marshals. At least 7—and these 7 are all members of the key decision-making bodies of the Central Committee, have had full military training and enjoy high ranking flag officer status, although they have not been on extended active duty.

Brezhnev is a good example, for he holds the rank of Lt. General and was formerly military-political officer in the Ministry of Defense.

Dimitriy Ustinov is a prime example. He holds the rank of Lt. General, graduated from the Military-Industrial Institute, has spent his life in the armaments industry and is now responsible in the Central Committee for planning and operational supervision of the *entire military-industrial structure of the U.S.S.R.* He is the Czar of Russian military-industrial power. He is a key member of the Central Committee and all important decisions of this body relative to the "building of the Armed Forces" pass over his desk in one form or another.

Central Committee Members M. S. Solomentsev, V. A. Kirilenko, N. D. Savinkin, and A. Yepishev have all had extensive military or

---

7. Sosnovy, *Foreign Affairs*, July 1966, page 1.

✦

industrial experience in the U.S.S.R. as have many other members of the Central Committee.

The heavy concentration of military, technical, and industrial experience and the direct participation of a large number of active military officers in the highest decision-making agencies of the Soviet Union is an important feature of the U.S.S.R. war economy. High-level military requirements decisions and military strategy decisions are reached in the Soviet Union with the benefit of strong military-technical and industrial judgments.

Whereas many voices in the U.S. call for cuts in the defense budgets and large new expenditures for social reconstruction programs, the Soviet Union is able to devote the lion's share of its economic resources to weapons systems while holding expenditures for the domestic sector to very low levels. The Soviet leaders are taking resources that should go for housing, food and other needs and wants and devoting them to military programs.

Former Secretary of Defense Clark Clifford, in preparing the 1970 defense budget, noted that "for the Soviets even to attempt to keep pace in a renewed strategic arms race of large proportions would be enormously costly for them in financial terms, and it would divert badly needed resources from the civilian sector of the economy."

What Secretary Clifford failed to add, however, was that the Soviets not only can keep pace in strategic weaponry—but are outpacing the United States—because they exercise overall control over the economy and can suppress public opposition that might arise. Such is the nature of the Communist system of control.

In the United States, on the other hand, the needs of national defense can be obscured or delayed by emphasis on domestic needs or wants.

Research and Development

One of the most critical areas in which to compare effort lies in military research and development.

Dr. Timothy Sosnovy of the Library of Congress estimates that 85 percent of the Soviet research and development effort is militarily oriented. In equivalent dollars (one *research* ruble buys what $2.75 would buy in the U.S. market), he estimates that the total 1968 U.S.S.R. military R&D budget was $23.1 billion. This is substantially higher than the Stanford Research Institute figures but it is compatible with Mr. Kozlowski's analysis.[8]

---

8. Library of Congress, ATD report, 69-48-116-1, Timothy Sosnovy, Ph.D., "Research and Development in the Soviet Union Today", 21 January 1969, p. 88.

The goal of Soviet research is world-wide military technological superiority.

This is not a new goal—Stalin established it clearly in 1948 when he said that the U.S.S.R would achieve technical superiority over capitalistic nations.

Brezhnev reiterated the goal at a meeting in the Kremlin of military academy graduates and Party and Government leaders which was reported in *Pravda*, July 2, 1968:

> "Science and technology have made it possible to create a powerful, qualitative new material and technical base.

> "Our superiority in the latest types of military technology is a fact, comrades, and one cannot escape facts."

There is reason to believe that a very large percentage of U.S.S.R. investment in military R&D is focused on basic research. The importance of this, of course, is that breakthroughs come most rapidly from basic research. Thus, heavy U.S.S.R. investments in strategic forces are supported by strong investments for new technology for new systems which, the Soviets hope, will continue to favorably influence the Soviet strategic lead.

Education Emphasis

The United States needs to consider increasing its strength in the area of intellectual resources, especially with respect to technical education. This need becomes apparent when we compare U.S./U.S.S.R. technical and scientific graduates.

The foundation of military power today is technical education. Figure 2 shows a comparison of U.S.S.R. and U.S.A. Scientific and Engineering Graduates. The U.S. College and University enrollment is substantially greater than that of the Soviet Union. However, the emphasis in the U.S.S.R. is placed on technical education and the number of science and engineering graduates annually is continuing to increase. In 1967, the U.S.S.R. produced some 220,000 graduates compared to some 36,000 graduates in the United States. (See Figure 2)

Indications are that the Soviets passed us in total R&D manpower, but if we discount the number of U.S. R&D personnel who work wholly in the consumer production industries, the Soviets probably had more military R&D manpower than we had as early as 1958-1959. Trends indicate that the Soviet R&D manpower pool will continue to increase through 1980. Since most of the Soviet engineering graduates available today received their degrees in the last fifteen years, the R&D manpower of the Soviet Union is young and perhaps

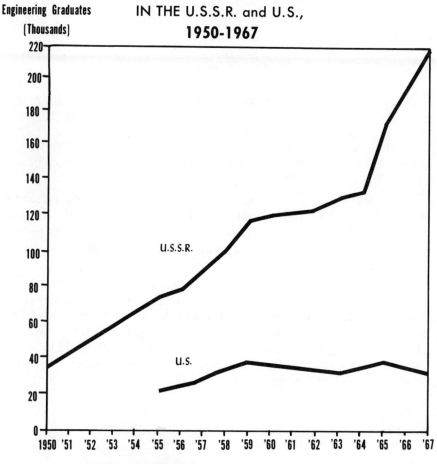

COMPARISON OF NUMBERS OF
SCIENTIFIC AND ENGINEERING GRADUATES
IN THE U.S.S.R. and U.S.,
1950-1967

SOURCES: HEW STUDIES
DR. TIMOTHY SOSNOVY, RESEARCH AND DEVELOPMENT
IN THE SOVIET UNION
LIBRARY OF CONGRESS, SURVEYS IN FOREIGN S&T LITERATURE
(SEE TEXT FOR DETAIL)

Figure 2

33

bolder than older men would be. Similarly, because the overall Soviet skilled manpower pool is growing rapidly, Soviet R&D capabilities will increase in ability to tackle complex new technologies and systems applications.

The comparative results of these contrasting policies can be seen in the following table:

Total Number of Engineers and Scientists [9]

	U.S.	U.S.S.R.
1940	297,000	295,000
1950	404,000	400,000
1960	796,000	1,135,000
1965	965,000	1,631,000
1966	996,000	1,789,000
1967	1,025,000	1,960,000
1968	1,055,000	2,120,000

It should be carefully noted, however, that the quality of training received by some of these Soviet scientists and engineers is inferior to that in the United States.

This year, the U.S. Government reduced support to education, especially to graduate education. This was a potentially harmful decision, unless graduate training can be stimulated indirectly through increased investments in research, development, testing and production work.

If the United States intends to remain competitive in science and technology in the markets of the world, the national support of advanced education in these areas must be substantially increased. This support will have to extend to the development of actions necessary to interest American students in pursuing technical areas of education, for there has been a serious decline in student interest in science and technology during the past two or three years.

---

9. Dr. T. Sosnovy, *op. cit.* p. 74.

CHAPTER III

THE CHANGED STRATEGIC MILITARY BALANCE

In the preceding section we considered the relative investments of the U.S.A. and U.S.S.R. in strategic forces. In this section, we will consider the effects on the relative balance of strategic forces.

A previous subcommittee of the National Strategy Committee of the American Security Council concluded in its 1967 study entitled, "The Changing Strategic Balance, U.S.A./U.S.S.R. that:

> "The preponderance of evidence points to the conclusion that the Soviet Union is succeeding in its massive drive toward strategic superiority and that the United States is cooperating in this effort by slowing down its side of the arms race."

On the basis of the following examination of the trends since then, we find that the earlier subcommittee's conclusion was accurate.

1969 ICBM Balance

How the situation has changed since 1967 can be illustrated, in numerical terms. In a comparative summary of missile strength, former Secretary of Defense Clark Clifford stated in his January 15, 1969 Posture Statement that the United States had 1,054 intercontinental ballistic missiles (ICBMs) and the Soviets had 900 ICBMs on September 1, 1968.

On March 19, Secretary of Defense Laird testified to the Senate Committee on Armed Services:

> "As of today, the Soviets have in being and under construction more ICBM launchers than the 1,048 possessed by the United States."

On April 25, 1969 Secretary Laird reported the Soviet ICBM total as 1140. This includes 1,000 ICBMs in hardened sites and 140 ICBMs on launching pads.[10] He also said that the Soviets could have 2500 ICBMs by 1975.

The New York *Times*, in an analysis of Soviet weaponry (April 14, 1969) said:

> "Qualified sources say that the new evidence gathered by high-flying satellites shows that the Soviet Union has about 1,200 intercontinental ballistic missiles in place or rapidly going into place, roughly 150 more land-based ICBMs than the United States."

On April 10, 1969, the Institute for Strategic Studies (London) released a study which concluded that: "The Soviet Union must now

---

10. New York *Times*, April 26, 1969, p. 1.

be treated as a full equal in terms both of strategic power and of her ability to control conflict in the developing world." [11]

Deputy Secretary of Defense David Packard, in testimony before the Senate Armed Services Committee March 20, 1969, stated:

> "One of the things that impressed me very much in the studies that I have made is that we have a good deal of evidence, quite hard evidence, that the Soviet ICBM deployment and development is continuing. It was this that caused us to take another hard look as to what we should do about this ABM capability."

Fundamental to the understanding of this dramatic change is the erroneous assumption of U.S. policy-makers in recent years that the Soviet Union would not seek a superior offensive capability but would seek parity. This error imposed American assumptions on our vision of Soviet strategy. As a result the Soviets now enjoy a widening advantage. This was underlined by Deputy Secretary Packard on March 20 when he told the Senate Armed Services Committee in analyzing charts of Soviet missile strength:

> "As you can see, parity has been reached. The smaller Soviet missiles represented in this area of the chart make up the larger part of the totals. Those large missiles that have the accuracy and yield to be a threat to our Minuteman forces are projected on the larger part of the figure. They became operational in 1966 and their inventory has grown . . . These are the large missiles on which the Soviets have flown multiple warheads. Thus, this force potentially represents a severe threat to our Minuteman."

Using the data provided by Deputy Secretary Packard and using official Defense Department statistics, the comparative ICBM trends appear in Figure 3.

Of special concern is the Soviet development and deployment of a very heavy intercontinental ballistic missile, the SS-9, which was unknown to the U.S. public until it was disclosed by Secretary Laird in his initial appearance this Spring before the Senate Armed Services Committee. This missile carries a warhead in the range of 20-25 megatons, far larger than anything in the U.S. inventory. Because of its size and its accuracy, the SS-9 is regarded as a weapon designed to knock out American Minuteman ICBM's.

The figures indicate that former Secretary of Defense McNamara's assessment in his defense posture statement in 1968 that,

> "the Soviet ICBM force will continue to grow over the next few years, but at a considerably smaller rate than in the recent past,"

---

11. Washington Post, April 11, 1969 article by Alfred Friendly.

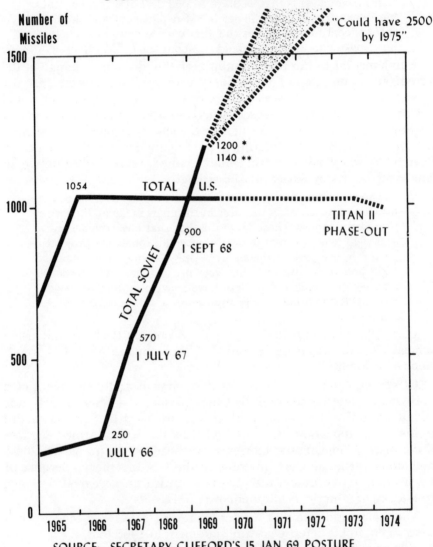

COMPARATIVE
U.S. SOVIET ICBM STRENGTH

Number of
Missiles

** "Could have 2500
by 1975"

1500

1200 *
1140 **

1054   TOTAL   U.S.

1000

TITAN II
PHASE-OUT

900
I SEPT 68

TOTAL SOVIET

570
I JULY 67

500

250
IJULY 66

0

1965   1966   1967   1968   1969   1970   1971   1972   1973   1974

SOURCE: SECRETARY CLIFFORD'S 15 JAN 69 POSTURE
STATEMENT AND PREVIOUS SECRETARY OF
DEFENSE POSTURE STATEMENTS. (SEE TEXT FOR DETAIL)
*NEW YORK TIMES, 14 APR 69
**SECRETARY LAIRD, 25 APR 69

Figure 3

COMPARISON OF
SUB LAUNCHED MISSILE STRENGTH

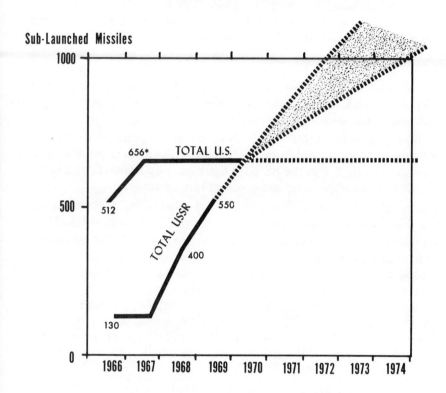

Sub-Launched Missiles

656*   TOTAL U.S.

512

TOTAL USSR   550

400

130

1000

500

0

1966   1967   1968   1969   1970   1971   1972   1973   1974

SOURCES: MILITARY BALANCE 1968-69
THE INSTITUTE OF STRATEGIC STUDIES, LONDON
CENTER FOR STRATEGIC STUDIES, STUDY ON SOVIET
NAVAL POWER (TO BE PUBLISHED)
(SEE TEXT FOR DETAIL)

*INCLUDES 496 POSEIDON AND 160 POLARIS

Figure 4

was not correct. President Nixon emphasized our faulty intelligence estimates when he noted during his press conference on April 18, 1969 that production of SS-9 missiles and nuclear submarines has been 60 percent greater than was estimated in 1967 when the decision was first made to deploy the Sentinel ABM system.

The present Soviet ICBM force now includes well over 200 SS-9s and this deployment is progressing at a fairly rapid rate—particularly since December 1968. This is the missile which is projected by the Defense Department to reach possibly 500 by 1975. This missile booster can also be adapted to fire an orbital bombardment warhead. It can also be adapted to carry a multiple warhead, which the Soviets are known to have been testing. With reference to Soviet testing it is noteworthy that one such Soviet test into the Pacific Ocean was made public by Secretary of State Rogers on April 12, 1969. He stated that the Soviet Union had tested the multiple warhead before but that this recent test was a "longer shot."

In addition to the SS-9, the Soviets are continuing to deploy the SS-11 and the newer SS-13 model ICBMs. These carry smaller warheads than the SS-9, but the SS-13 is the first solid-fueled Soviet ICBM and it can be developed and deployed in large numbers.

This surge in Soviet ICBMs is one of the most direct reasons for the Nixon Administration decision to proceed with the Safeguard ABM.

The urgency of a defensive capability against ballistic missiles is underscored by the increasing confidence of Soviet leaders that they can build up their offensive capabilities with less fear of detection by U.S. space reconnaissance vehicles. This is indicated by a recent statement by Marshal Kirill Moskalenko, former Commander-in-Chief of Soviet Strategic Rocket Troops, later promoted to and now serving as Soviet Deputy Minister of Defense. The official Soviet news agency TASS quoted Deputy Defense Minister Moskalenko on February 19, 1969 as having stated that,

> "mobile compexes for launching intercontinental hard-fuel missiles are the most important latest features. These complexes have high maneuverability, can be well camouflaged, and therefore cannot be spotted by the enemy's aerial or space reconnaissance. Some of the latest Soviet rockets are suitable for orbital launching."

The U.S.S.R. has built some eight types of ICBMs in the last 10 years (SS-6 through SS-13). Soviet investments in missile research, design, development and test have been adequate to produce a *new* ICBM every year or two. We should, therefore, expect to see new models in the future until we see a fundamental change in Soviet investment in military systems.

1969 Orbital Bombardment Balance

The Soviets presently enjoy a clear lead in space orbital weapons. Mr. McNamara released information in 1967 that the U.S.S.R. was developing a fractional orbital bombardment system. Mr. Laird confirmed that the Soviets were very likely deploying this system. He said:

> "They are also working hard on FOBS . . . also designed to reduce warning time to our bombers so that they will not have sufficient time to become airborne." (testimony March 20)

If these vehicles were launched into near earth orbit on approximately 70-75° inclination, they would bracket the United States periodically. (They would then be known as Orbital Bombardment Systems rather than FOBS.) Properly deployed, a significant number, let us say 100, could be in a position to attack the United States in a matter of seconds after the button was pushed in the Kremlin. This would add enormously to a credible Soviet capability to execute a first strike against the United States.

1969 Submarine Launched Missile (SLM) Balance

In his testimony before the Senate Armed Services Committee on March 19, Deputy Defense Secretary Packard commented on Soviet submarine launched missiles:

> "We know that the Soviets have been moving ahead with a rather active program in producing Polaris-type submarines. They are now in production. They are not yet deployed as far as we know. But this gives the Soviets the possibility of launching missiles from locations close to our shores, and we are very much concerned about this threat which could reduce the ability of our bombing force to get off."

The submarine referred to here is the "Y" class, which went into production in 1968. Seven were commissioned in that year and the Soviets have a production capability now estimated at one per month. This sub carries 16 underwater-launched, 1500-mile range missiles. Secretary of the Navy Chafee, in his testimony to the Senate Committee referred to it when he declared that,

> "The Soviets are modernizing their submarine force, the world's largest. Following a period of large-scale shipyard expansion, new classes of ballistic missile submarine and nuclear attack boats are becoming operational. More of these new types have been launched than foreseen a year ago."

In its comparison of strategic nuclear forces between the U.S. and the U.S.S.R. the Defense Department credits the U.S.S.R. with 45 deployable SLBMs on September 1, 1968 compared with 656 U.S. Polaris missiles on the same date.

These figures, however, are incomplete as indicators of comparative strength because they included only the first two of the new nuclear-powered "Y" and 10 of the older "H" class (three missiles each). They did not include Soviet ballistic missiles mounted on some 25 diesel-powered "G" class submarines (two missiles each), nor do they include the large number of submarine-launched cruise missiles. The official explanation is that these missiles are estimated to be targeted against strategic European land targets and against shipping, respectively. However, they could just as easily be targeted against U.S. cities and installations along our coasts. We include both categories in Figure 4 which shows existing and projected U.S./U.S.S.R. SLM strength. The Georgetown Center for Strategic Studies, in a forthcoming study, estimates total Soviet submarine-launched ballistic missiles at over 200 in March 1969 and cruise-type missiles at 350. In his Congressional testimony, Deputy Secretary Packard indicated that if the Soviets employ their maximum production rate for "Y" class submarines then their Polaris-type missiles alone could exceed the U.S. total of 656 by the end of Fiscal Year 1971.

In considering potential Soviet counterforce weapons such as the SS-9 missile, we should bear in mind the naval counterforce weapons— such as the fast attack submarines ("V" class)—that the Soviets are developing apparently for use against U.S. Polaris submarines, a vital component in nuclear defense.

The Institute for Strategic Studies (London) recently pointed out that the Soviet undersea fleet now exceeds in numbers all the submarines in the fleets of the United States and other NATO nations. The situation regarding attack submarines is critical and rapidly deteriorating. The Soviet Navy has more than a 2 to 1 numerical advantage over the U.S. Navy in this area of sea warfare, and this is a matter of concern since the attack submarine is considered to be the most effective weapon against a nuclear submarine. The U.S. position is worsened by the age of many of the attack boats. Forty-five of the 105 attack submarines in the U.S. Navy are of World War II construction. On the other hand, almost all of the Soviet attack submarines have been built within the last 14 years. It is these submarines that pose a direct threat to the U.S. ballistic missile-firing submarines.[12]

---

12. See also the "Changing Strategic Naval Balance, U.S.S.R. vs. U.S.A." prepared by the American Security Council for the House Armed Services Committee and released in Committee print December 5, 1968.

1969 MRBM/IRBM Balance

Former Secretary of Defense, Clark M. Clifford did not include the medium and intermediate range Soviet ballistic missiles in his 1969 Posture Statement assessment of the U.S.S.R. strategic inventory. The United States has no such weapons deployed against Soviet targets, whereas the Soviets have their missiles targeted against our NATO allies. He credited the U.S.S.R. with 700 operational MRBM/IRBM launchers, some in hardened sites. He declared that,

> "evidence is accumulating that the Soviets have embarked on the development of solid-fuel missiles for medium and intermediate as well as intercontinental ranges."

British Defense Minister Dennis Healy recently estimated that the Soviet MRBM/IRBM force now approximates 1,000 missiles.

1969 Bomber Balance

The United States continues to lead the Soviet Union in heavy bombers (B-52s and B-58s vs. Soviet Bisons and Bears), but Department of Defense figures show the U.S. ahead overall in bomber strength only because the Soviet Badger and Blinder medium range bombers are not credited with a strategic role. Both their threat to Western Europe or their threat to the continental U.S.—they are air refuelable—makes them strategic bombers.

Figure 5 gives comparable U.S. and U.S.S.R. bomber strengths and trends. Seventeen squadrons of U.S. B-52G-H bombers will be modified with the SRAM air to surface missile by Fiscal 1971 and will be retained in service, along with 80 B-58s and some of the B-52C-Fs.

It is not yet clear whether the U.S.S.R. will replace its heavy bombers (Bisons and Bears) or the medium bombers. However, they have provided these bombers with air to surface missiles which will extend their lives considerably. Air Force Chief of Staff McConnell testified before the Senate Armed Services Committee that Soviet "production continues on a supersonic dash medium bomber and a reconnaissance version of a heavy bomber is being manufactured in limited numbers." Air Force Secretary Seamans also testified that "the Soviets have some 200" heavy bombers. This figure exceeds Secretary Clifford's U.S. estimate of 150 Bison/Bear bombers.

The phase down of U.S. bombers could be reversed by adopting new aircraft or significantly modifying present ones.

Comparative Innovation Policies

Not only has the military power of the Soviet Union grown more rapidly than that of the U.S.A., but it has rapidly overtaken the forces of the United States in new concepts and new weapons systems.

COMPARISON OF BOMBERS

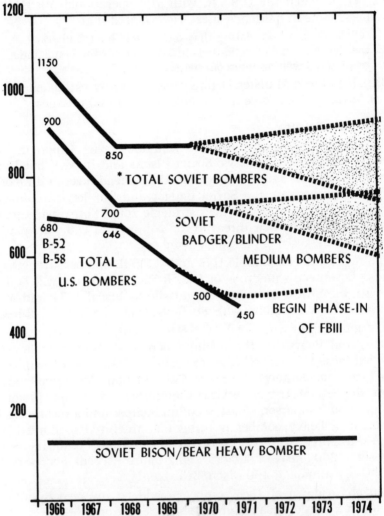

* ALL 1969 FIGURES AND TRENDS FROM FORMER SECRETARY CLIFFORD'S
15 JAN 69 POSTURE STATEMENT AND A.F. SECRETARY SEAMAN'S APRIL 16
TESTIMONY TO SENATE ARMED SERVICES COMMITTEE.

SECRETARY CLIFFORD REPORTED 150 U.S.S.R. HEAVY BOMBERS.

WE'VE USED LOWER FIGURE. EARLIER FIGURES FROM INSTITUTE FOR
STRATEGIC STUDIES, LONDON   (SEE TEXT FOR DETAIL)

Figure 5

The U.S.S.R. now has whole families of military (and naval) weapons systems that the United States does not have in its inventory:

1. The large IRBM and MRBM force (1000) is such a family of weapon systems. This force is primarily aimed at Europe and now completely pins Europe down. Generals of the U.S.S.R. have stated "we now hold Europe as a hostage."

2. Very large—50-100 megaton nuclear weapons which were tested in 1961-1962 and which, it is generally conceded in unclassified literature, have been adapted for missile delivery. The United States not only has no such weapons in its inventory—it has not even tested them and can only speculate as to the unique effects they may produce.

   In this connection, it should be noted that the Proton satellite, according to Soviet releases, weighed some 40,000 pounds. The Proton booster, therefore, could launch very large ICBM warheads (50 megaton) or large warhead orbital bombardment systems.

3. The Bear Bomber is unique. It is the world's longest range, highest endurance bomber. It is an effective anti-shipping and anti-submarine attack aircraft with air-to-surface attack missiles on board.

4. The ABM development and deployment in Russia is an innovation. This is discussed in detail later.

5. The orbital bombardment system is described elsewhere, but the U.S. has no counterpart. The U.S. respects the treaty forbidding the use of space for weapons of mass destruction.

Innovative policies in the U.S.S.R. are designed to exploit identifiable counterforce opportunities, whether offensive or defensive. The five we have mentioned are examples of many we could have mentioned, such as the world's largest helicopters, helicopter carriers, the world's first supersonic transport (which provides technology for a new heavy bomber) and others. With a firm counterforce strategy supported by positive innovative policies, the U.S.S.R. is developing a whole array of new military weapons which have no counterpart in the U.S. arsenal.

1969 Strategic Missile Balance

It is apparent that the Soviets have jumped into the lead in overall strategic missile strength. They have made optimum use of a much smaller economic base than the United States—in effect, they have been and are operating on a war economy basis.

The combined total of ICBMs, IR/MRBMs and SLMs is now esti-mated as 2,750 for the U.S.S.R. to 1,710 for the U.S.A. —See Figure 6.

Meanwhile, the "four-to-one" U.S. lead in individually targeted warheads, which was long used by the Defense Department as a source of reassurance to the American public, was discarded by Air Force Secretary, Dr. Robert C. Seamans, Jr., in his testimony to the Senate Armed Services Committee April 16, 1969:

> "The much-quoted figure of a 4-to-1 U.S. advantage in individually targetable warheads may not be too reassuring. The 4-to-1 figure stems mainly from the bomber portion of the forces, since missile forces are rapidly approaching a 1-to-1 relationship. It was arrived at by omitting the Soviet medium bomber force from the calculations, while counting several bombs on each of our own bombers. The inclusion of Soviet medium bombers, medium-range missiles, and cruise missile submarines would bring the ratio of individually targeted warheads close to 1-to-1, with a payload advantage somewhat in favor of the Soviets.

> "I might add that it is not enough to argue that these ratios involve relatively higher numbers, about 4,000 weapons on each side at the present time, and that only a few hundred weapons would be needed to destroy the Soviet Union. The critical factor here is not how many total weapons we have, but how many would survive a Soviet attack, and, of these, how many would penetrate Soviet defenses."

It should also be considered that Secretary Laird told the Senate Foreign Relations Committee that because of geography and the location of major centers of population and industry in Russia, as compared with the United States, *the U.S. needs to be able to deliver six times as many warheads as would the Russians to achieve destruction "parity" with them.*

It would take, he reported, some 1,200 one-megaton warheads to destroy 45 percent of the total population of Russia while the Soviet Union would need only 200 warheads of identical size to wipe out 55 percent of our population.

THE STRATEGIC DEFENSE

> ". . . one of the cardinal tasks for Soviet military strategy is the reliable protection of the country from nuclear strikes, anti-missile and air defense."

> *Military Strategy,* edited by Marshal of the Soviet Union V. D. Sokolovsky.

COMPARISON OF TOTAL STRATEGIC MISSILES
(ICBM, SLM, MRBM/IRBM)

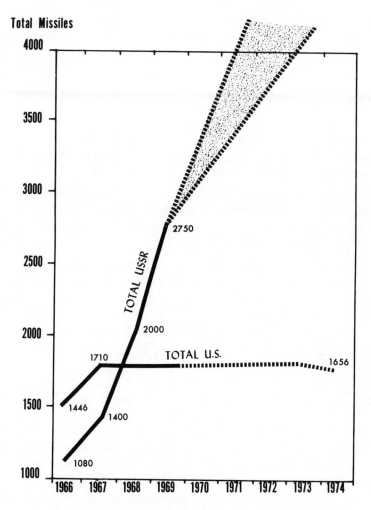

SOURCES: COMPENDIUM OF SECRETARY CLIFFORD'S POSTURE
STATEMENT, 15 JAN 69

INSTITUTE OF STRATEGIC STUDIES
"MILITARY BALANCE 1968-69"

(SEE TEXT FOR DETAIL)

Figure 6

The Soviets always have devoted great attention to active defense as a key component of their military policy. As Dr. D. G. Brennan, Director of the Hudson Institute has pointed out (p. 12 Adelphia Papers, Nov. 1967), "This heavy doctrinal bias in favor of defense can probably be traced to Russian military experience at least as far back as Napoleon. It is the Soviets who initiated ballistic missile defense deployment."

Against this background of Soviet thinking one can trace the manner in which the Soviet Union has developed strategic defense forces.

While the United States conducts a national debate over deployment of the Safeguard anti-missile system, it is worthwhile noting that the genesis of the Soviet ABM system dates from the early 1950s. With three generations of ABM weapons already developed, and a fourth under test, the Soviets are now in a position to deal with the far more sophisticated problems of defense against space weapons. Even if the Safeguard ABM system is approved by Congress, the Soviet Union still will enjoy a sizeable lead in strategic defense.

From the first, the Soviets have given strategic defense the command recognition it deserves in the nuclear era.

The New Defense Service—P-V-O

In 1954, the Kremlin's top military and political planners decided to create a military service equal in status to the Army, Navy and Air Force. Since then, the Soviet Union has been moving ahead in development of nuclear age defenses. The new service was named P-V-O Strany for the Russian words *protivo-vozdushnaya oborona strany*, meaning "anti-air defense of the country."

Initially, P-V-O consisted largely of World War II fighters, anti-aircraft artillery, and radars—many of which the United States gave the U.S.S.R. under wartime lend-lease, such as the SCR 584. Its first commander was the World War II hero of the defense of Leningrad, Marshal L. A. Govsov. P-V-O grew rapidly. The MIG-15, the MIG-17, the MIG-19, the MIG-21 and, most recently, the MIG-23, the Foxbat— have all been built and deployed extensively (Foxbat is just being deployed) all over the U.S.S.R. and her satellites.

In April of this year, a new book, *"Fifty Years of the Armed Forces of the U.S.S.R."* arrived in the United States for registration at the U.S. Library of Congress.

Published last year, it was written by Marshal M. V. Zakharov, Chief of the General Staff of the Soviet Armed Forces. In it, he recalls that in 1958, P-V-O began taking on new dimensions:

"The creation of ballistic missiles and space vehicles required a modern air defense system to respond not only against the aircraft threat, but also—*and first of all*—to provide anti-missile and anti-space (specifically, in Russian, anti-cosmic) defense."

Soviet scientists, engineers, designers and industrialists were mobilized to provide a new subdivision called P-R-O (*protivo-raketnaya oborona*, or ABM, literally anti-rocket defense), while the original responsibilities of P-V-O were turned over to a new subdivision, P-S-O (*protivo-samoletnaya oborona*, or anti-aircraft defense).

P-R-O missiles were first deployed in 1963 and have since been increased in number and improved.

The Soviet Union officially describes P-R-O's mission as the

". . . interception and destruction of enemy missiles or rockets in space, preferably at distant approaches to their objectives and far from national territory." [13]

P-R-O first relied on a so-called "point defense" not unlike, but far less sophisticated than, the Safeguard system requested by the Nixon Administration for protection of a few selected sites where our retalitory Minuteman intercontinental ballistic missiles are installed.

As the Russians viewed "point" defense, P-R-O was set up around their ICBM strategic weapons bases, key military command centers, and most vital industrial complexes. This system soon was enlarged to provide area defense rather than just "point" defense.

The Soviet Union has built a belt (often referred to as the "Blue Belt" defense system) defense ranging from the Baltic Coast and named for one of the anchors in the line—the city of Tallinn, capital of Estonia. Marshal Malinovsky reported the completion of this belt defense system to the 23rd Congress of the Communist Party of the Soviet Union. At that time he described it as being "for the defense of the entire territory of the Soviet Union."

P-V-O has set up regional command centers throughout the Soviet Union and the border areas of its satellites where both P-R-O and P-S-O units are stationed. However, the only known regional deployment of P-R-O missiles is around the metropolitan complex of Moscow.

Recent news accounts indicate there are some 67 P-R-O missile sites around the Russian capital.

P-V-O has established six command centers in Eastern European satellites—one each in Bulgaria, Czechoslovakia, East Germany, Hun-

---

13. "Troops of National Air Defense" (1968), book by Marshall P. F. Batitsky.

gary, Poland, and Rumania. In addition, there are 14 command centers in the Soviet Union.

P-V-O operations with the satellite countries are completely integrated under a Warsaw Pact three-star Russian general who operates from a headquarters of the Russian national P-V-O command. Thus, P-V-O like all other military operations in the Soviet bloc, is totally integrated under Russian control. Marshal Zakharov writes further in his book:

"The troops of P-V-O Strany consist of surface-to-air missile units, fighter aviation, radio-technical troops and missile-carrying aircraft. Surface-to-air missile troops are the new branch (P-R-O) of the P-V-O troops . . . equipped with combat missile complexes of differing purposes and capability. . . .

"The characteristic element of these missiles is the fact that they are guided in flight which permits directing the missile to the target area and homing it on the target for its complete destruction. The aiming of missiles is accomplished by means of complex automatic computerized guidance systems. The target is destroyed as a rule by the first launched missile. The modern surface-to-air missile complexes are capable of destruction of all existing types of planes and missiles the enemy possesses at this time. . . .

"The surface-to-air missile troops are constantly undergoing developmental improvements. New families and generations of missiles are created with improved and perfected combat qualities and alert capabilities. The range of operations, speed of launching and all other operational characteristics of P-R-O missiles are constantly being improved."

Thus, with pride and assurance to the Russian people does the Soviet Chief of Staff claim ABM progress over the past ten years in the Soviet Union. Marshal Zakharov's words may be discarded by critics of anti-missile defense, but the fact remains the Soviets have ABM forces in being and the United States does not. No U.S. Commander can similarly assure the American people that they have such a defense against nuclear war. Moreover, the Soviet ABM becomes more significant as Soviet offensive power increases. Air Force Secretary Seamans testified on April 16 that:

"The effect of accurate Soviet MIRVs would be compounded by an expanded Soviet ABM system. If a Soviet MIRV attack could destroy a considerable portion of U.S. retaliatory forces, the remaining U.S. missiles might be unable to overcome the Soviet ABM defense."

Space Defense

The present commander-in-chief of P-V-O is Marshal P. F. Batitsky, who took over in 1966. His responsibility for P-R-O and the conventional P-S-O anti-aircraft defenses has been expanded to include the establishment of an entirely new field mentioned earlier by Marshal Zakharov as anti-space defense. This subdivision of P-V-O is labeled P-K-O (*protivo-kosmicheskaya oborona*, Russian for defense against space-orbiting combat missiles or intelligence (spy) satellites).

Such space defense may have three objectives: 1) To be able to neutralize or destroy U.S. reconnaissance satellites which presently are our prime source of information about Soviet strategic deployment; 2) to develop a means of neutralizing or destroying our intercontinental ballistic missiles shortly after they are launched; 3) to gain control of space. There have been numerous references in Soviet speeches and official documents to indicate such an objective.

Evidence of a Soviet test of anti-space defense was provided by a report, released in the mid-April *Satellite Situation Report* published by the U.S. Air Defense Command. That document disclosed that between October 19 and the first of November 1968, three space vehicles were launched by the Soviet Union from their Cape Kennedy, known as the Tyuratam Space Center.

Cosmos satellite 248 was sent into orbit on a trajectory that would carry it to an angle of 62.2° over the Equator. On practically the same course, Cosmos 249 and 252 were sent after it. About 300 miles above earth, the three satellites were in close proximity. Suddenly, 249 and 252 exploded into little pieces, according to the U.S. report. Cosmos 248, unharmed, continued on its way.

The explosion of the two satellites was non-nuclear, according to the *Satellite Situation Report*.

The Soviet Union's emphasis on an anti-missile system was demonstrated on April 14, 1969 when Warsaw Pact forces conducted their first Spring maneuvers. Marshal Batitsky, who holds the post of Air Defense Commander for the Warsaw Pact, as well as that of chief of P-V-O, was placed in charge of the maneuvers which were described as an effort to improve "anti-aircraft" defenses, but reportedly involved much more than a defense against conventional weapons or vehicles.

It is clear that P-V-O structures including P-R-O, P-S-O and P-K-O, enjoy a high priority in Soviet military planning.

ABM Research and Development

Figure 7 shows a time plot of new Soviet surface-to-air (anti-aircraft, anti-missile, and anti-space) missiles.

SOVIET
DEFENSIVE MISSILE DEVELOPMENTS

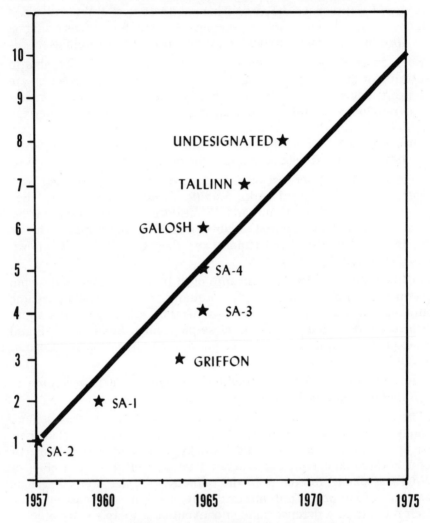

SOURCES: APPEARANCE OF RESPECTIVE SYSTEMS
INSTITUTE OF STRATEGIC STUDIES,
MILITARY BALANCE 1968-'69
JANES ALL THE WORLD AIRCRAFT

(SEE TEXT FOR DETAIL)

Figure 7

The Soviets are developing a new surface-to-air missile roughly every year to 18 months.

This means that the U.S.S.R. has made consistent and steady investments in research and development forces to create ABM systems.

So, if the present Galosh and Tallinn systems are not wholly effective in the judgment of the U.S.S.R., new systems will undoubtedly appear which will improve the effectiveness of the overall Soviet ABM system.

Other Defenses

While the Soviet Union is developing the most sophisticated forms of strategic defense, it is not neglecting more basic types of defense. Thus it is making full use of manned aircraft and anti-air artillery.

Some 4,000 P-V-O fighters including the MIG-17, 19, and 21, and the newer all-weather YAK-28 Firebars, and YAK-42 are now deployed in this system. New Foxbat (MIG-23) fighters, probably the best fighters in the world, are joining the force at present.

No such fighter development has taken place in the United States. We are in serious need of meeting this obvious requirement by means of the early deployment of production aircraft tailored both to the defense of our shore bases and ships, as well as to the fighter-to-fighter mission. Our latest and best fighter, the F-4, was developed 15 years ago and is destined to comprise the bulk of our fighter inventory for five to 10 more years.

We have not found the number of anti-aircraft artillery deployed in the U.S.S.R. and Satellites in the unclassified literature. However, if the extremely dense deployment of AA guns in North Viet Nam is any index, it is reasonable to expect that Eastern Europe and the U.S.S.R. also are the sites of very dense anti-aircraft artillery positions. The artillery ranges from 23 mm guns to 130 mm guns.

It is also noteworthy that the U.S.S.R. has obtained valuable combat experience from the coordinated use of missiles and AA guns in North Vietnam. The surface-to-air missiles forced U.S. aircraft to fly at lower altitudes, thus exposing themselves to AA weapons.

No significant anti-aircraft artillery remains in U.S. forces. AAA has been largely retired. However, the continued effectiveness of AAA has been amply demonstrated by North Vietnamese forces.

Civil Defense is part of the respective strategic defense programs. It is so important, however, that we have made it the subject of a separate section of this study.

CHAPTER IV

CIVIL DEFENSE

The Soviets are developing a comprehensive civil defense program. The Soviets are spending about 10 times as much effort as is the United States in providing the Soviet society an adequate civil defense. Moreover, civil defense in the Soviet Union is related directly to overall Soviet military strategy. This is how one senior military general in the U.S.S.R. expressed it:

> "We have to be concerned with the enemy's nuclear strikes. However, one must keep in mind that the aggressors will not be able to make full use for their purposes of their strategic capabilities of attack. A portion of their means of weapon delivery will be destroyed or damaged already before they are launched, while still on their launch sites, bases, and air fields. Another portion will be destroyed or damaged by weapons of the Air Defense Forces while in flight at the approach to the territory of the Socialist camp; still another portion of missiles and aircraft will fail to reach their targets due to technical reasons. However, some portion of the chemical, biological, and nuclear weapons may reach their targets."

And he goes on to show that civil defense, being the "Defense of Motherland," will handle the few weapons that may reach targets.[14]

How will Soviet civil defense accomplish this?

In the first place, the U.S.S.R. has invested significant facility and personnel resources in civil defense. Figure 8 shows the estimated balance, U.S./U.S.S.R., in civil defense efforts. The U.S. data was provided by the DOD office of civil defense and is derived from annual budget figures together with a somewhat optimistic estimate of local efforts.

The U.S.S.R. data is derived from Leon Goure's work, from Joanne Levey's work, and are obviously broad estimates. We know of no definitive study of U.S./U.S.S.R. civil defense investments.

While the Soviet civil defense program represents a massive effort, it is not a crash program; its strength is cumulative, resulting from a steady attempt to expand and upgrade every facet since its inception, in its present form, in the early 1950's.

The basic objectives of the program are:

"(1) To safeguard the population from nuclear, chemical and bacteriological weapons;

"(2) To protect industrial installations and maintain production;

"(3) To protect agricultural resources; and

---

14. Lt. Gen. Shuvyrin, October 1968, "Military Knowledge," Moscow.

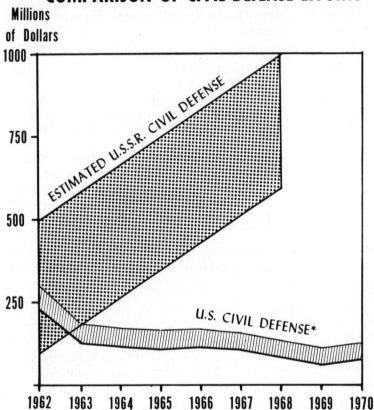

COMPARISON OF CIVIL DEFENSE EFFORTS

Millions
of Dollars

1000

ESTIMATED U.S.S.R. CIVIL DEFENSE

750

500

250

U.S. CIVIL DEFENSE*

1962 1963 1964 1965 1966 1967 1968 1969 1970

SOURCES:

U.S. DOD BUDGET FIGURES

LEON GOURÉ , CIVIL DEFENSE IN THE SOVIET UNION,
RAND 1963 (BEING UPDATED AT PRESENT)

OAK RIDGE NATIONAL LABORATORIES, JOANNE LEVY,
"CIVIL DEFENSE IN THE SOVIET UNION",
"SURVIVE", MARCH-APRIL 1969

*BOTTOM LINE IS DOD BUDGET FIGURE.

$50 MILLION IS ADDED ANNUALLY AS ESTIMATED
STATE AND LOCAL EFFORT.

(SEE TEXT FOR DETAIL)

Figure 8

"(4) To undertake massive rescue and reclamation operations to liquidate the effects of an attack as quickly as possible.

"More specifically, protection of the population is achieved by:

"(1) Building shelters;

"(2) Providing the population with individual means of protection (such as gas masks and protective clothing);

"(3) Evacuating the population in the event of escalating crisis;

"(4) Training the population to make use of the available means of protection;

"(5) Warning the population and the national economic establishment of attack;

"(6) Conducting rescue and repair operations in stricken areas;

"(7) Rendering medical aid to the injured; and

"(8) Preventing panic." [15]

The Soviets have no question about whether to build a civil defense or not. It is not a matter for debate. "People who have pulled incendiary bombs out by the fins and seen Red Square on fire and the Kremlin ablaze have been there before. They need no convincing." [16] In the

Soviet Union:

1. The entire population is being trained. Elementary school children in grades 5, 6, and 7 are taught 15 hours a year about civil defense. Then pre-draft age men, men in camps, and men in schools are trained. The farmers, factory workers—all Russians are trained to perform civil defense activities.

2. Heavy equipment such as bulldozers, cranes and shovels are stockpiled and civilians are taught to use them in an emergency.

3. Perhaps the most realistic and convincing part of the entire program is the development and realistic practicing of evacuation plans. These plans and exercises involve entire cities. Most impressive is the military-civilian organization that has been developed to plan, practice, and implement evacuation. Every city executive committee chairman is the local civil defense commander and his deputy is in charge of evacuation. Each city, factory, and collective

15. Joanne Levey, "Survive", March, April 1969. Mrs. Levey is participating in the Civil Defense Project at the Oak Ridge National Laboratories.
16. Ibid.

farm has a full-time civil defense military staff. These are supported by regional commands and a central command in Moscow under Marshal Chirikov.

4. Civil defense in the U.S.S.R. is planned against nuclear, biological, and chemical weapons. Industrial operations are especially protected.

5. An overriding feature of the Soviet program concentrates on the prevention of panic. An attempt is made to give a sense of personal responsibility for the protection of the Motherland to each citizen. Discipline, training, and morale of the people are stressed.

Overall, one is impressed with the serious attitude and demeanor of the people and the realism of the programs. There is, of course, the usual bad planning and the spotty performance one sees in Soviet activity, but the entire program is impressive.

In relative strategic balance, the program must be considered an advantage to the U.S.S.R.

> "Even more convincing than the assurance of survival to the Russian people is the attractive proposition held out by Kremlin leaders that hard-core civil defense strength on the home front means much more than realistic survival insurance: it means making nuclear attack on the Soviet Union unattractive, without requisite gain and full of unacceptable risk. *It means giving Red diplomats* a particularly effective weapon at the conference table. [17]

---

17. Joanne Levey . . . *op. cit.*

CHAPTER V

THE NEED FOR A MISSILE DEFENSE

"I believe it (the Safeguard ABM system) is absolutely essential for the security of the country . . . I do not want to see an American President in the future, in the event of a crisis, to have his diplomatic credibility be so impaired because the United States was in a second class or inferior position. We saw what it meant to the Soviets when they were second. I don't want that position to be the United States' in the event of a future diplomatic crisis."

> President Richard Nixon, Press Conference, April 18, 1969

On March 14, 1969, President Nixon announced that his Administration planned to modify the Sentinel missile defense system approved by Congress under the Johnson Administration by using it first to defend some U.S. retaliatory missiles rather than to defend cities. This modification was named the "Safeguard" system.

In the words of the President, "this measured deployment is designed to fulfill three objectives:

"1. Protection of our land-based retaliatory forces against a direct attack by the Soviet Union.

"2. Defense of the American people against the kind of nuclear attack which Communist China is likely to be able to mount within the decade.

"3. Protection against the possibility of accidental attacks from any source."

Two American presidents, representing our two major political parties, have now recommended to the American people that the United States needs a missile defense system.

The issue now squarely before the country is the Safeguard system. Unlike Sentinel, Safeguard has been modified so that its defensive intent is unmistakable. The first deployment is to cover only two missile sites, the first of which will not be completed before 1973. The present estimate of the total cost of installing the system is $6-7 billion. The President has asked for it in order that he or his successors hopefully will not be placed in a position where they can be blackmailed by our self-proclaimed Communist enemies.

Safeguard is a modest, limited proposal. It is subject to constant review, as conditions change.

Nevertheless, the Safeguard ABM has become the focus of a major national debate. It has become a symbolic issue with many. Some of those who oppose the emphasis given to national defense expenditures have clearly chosen Safeguard as the issue on which to join in opposition.

The Safeguard debate has thus assumed such importance that all major defense decisions in the future will very likely be prejudiced if Safeguard is rejected. If the opposition to a strong military posture by the United States can win on a "defense only" issue, other proposals to strengthen our strategic capabilities would have scant chance of gaining approval.

Our President has said the United States needs the Safeguard system. He is the man most responsible for the security of our country and most knowledgeable about the factors involved. We believe his judgment should be respected and accepted.

Since some of our citizens have challenged this judgment and the grounds upon which it is based, we will hereinafter consider the issue directly. In the preceding four sections we have considered the environment and the circumstances at the time during which the Safeguard decision is being made. We believe that the following points merit consideration:

1. The Soviet Union is still committed to World Domination.

There is no indication that the overall political objective of the Soviet Union has altered. That objective, in the words of the Soviet Communist Party, is "the triumph of Socialism and Communism on a world-wide scale." Whether one takes this to mean "world domination" by the U.S.S.R. or simply an extension of the socio-political-economic *system* of Communism is not the key question. The important fact is that the Soviet Union is deliberately attempting to expand its power, influence and authority throughout the world.

2. The principal military thrust of the U.S.S.R. is to develop a massive and superior capability for nuclear war.

Soviet military doctrine stresses the need for military-technical superiority. It stresses also the importance of striking first if nuclear war comes. Soviet policy conforms to doctrine. The U.S.S.R. has already exceeded the United States in numbers of ICBMs and in total strategic missile launchers. Furthermore, there is no indication that the Soviets will settle for present force levels. On the contrary, the evidence indicates that the Soviets are vigorously improving and adding to all components of their strategic forces.

a. Defense Secretary Laird has disclosed that the Soviets have developed the SS-9 intercontinental missile that is capable of carrying a warhead of 20 to 25 megatons—a destructive capacity far beyond anything in the U.S. arsenal. Not only have the Soviets developed this large nuclear armed rocket, but they are deploying them in large numbers (over 200 at present). It has become clear, therefore, that the SS-9 is a counter-force weapon that poses a threat to the U.S. Minuteman missiles—the missiles that are intended to guarantee peace and security for the American people. The Administration announcement that the U.S.S.R. is seeking a counter force capability should surprise no one since it is a perfectly logical defense policy and goal, historically pursued by most, if not all, nations. What would be surprising would be news that the U.S.S.R. had adopted such questionable and unproven concepts as "parity" or disarmament by emulation.

The destruction of the enemy's forces, the only real threat, has always been the principal military objective in war. If one side can destroy the other's forces it can then impose its will on its opponent without fear of retaliation or even risk of substantive losses. A counter force capability is, therefore, the most logical goal for any nation that accepts the possibility of having to actually fight either aggressively or defensively.

b. The U.S.S.R. is spending more than twice as much as the United States to build its strategic military strength. The U.S.S.R. is spending about $18 billion yearly or about 4 to 5 percent of its gross national product on strategic military forces. The U.S. strategic military budget is only $7.6 billion yearly, or less than 1 percent of its gross national product.

c. The U.S.S.R. is spending about $18 billion or some 4 to 5 percent of its gross national product on military research and development. The United States is spending about $16 billion or about 2 percent of its gross national product on military research and development. This is an especially meaningful comparison for the future because this is the effort which leads to break-through development of new weapons systems.

d. As a result of this substantial research and development effort, the U.S.S.R. is pushing hard on new frontiers of science where the United States has chosen not to compete. For example, the offensive space weapon arena has been virtually ceded to the U.S.S.R. As the relative strength of the United States declines, the Communists will have even more options available to them.

e. The Soviet Union is developing its defensive strategic forces at a steady pace which gives every indication that the Soviets are, or soon will be in a position to limit a retaliatory blow which the United States might deliver after absorbing the weight of a Soviet first strike.

An optimum counterforce capability or offensive force posture does not *necessarily* imply first strike intentions. But without a counterforce potential, a first strike would make little or no sense since it would merely result in equally damaging retaliation. A counterforce capability also provides the best prospects for damage limiting.

Effective damage limiting requires a counterforce posture, and this in turn includes not only the ability to destroy enemy forces before they are launched, but also to destroy them en route. A good ABM system is part of a counterforce posture. So are missiles and warheads accurate enough to target enemy ICBM sites, submarines and bases. If and when all of these goals are achieved, an inevitable by-product is a good first strike capability. The two are indivisible from a capability point of view—though not necessarily from the point of view of intentions.

This is the situation towards which the Soviets are now building. They may not *intend* an actual attack on the United States in the sense of *preventive* war. We do not conclude that the Soviets *want* nuclear war. But they are preparing for every contingency, *including* nuclear war, and however it may come, they intend to get in the first blow, according to their own doctrine.

In the Soviet view, a failure to take advantage of an historical opportunity is a crime. Such an opportunity was presented to the Soviets in the 1960s by the unilateral action of the United States in holding back its side of the strategic arms race. *Political utility* is the key point in making use of capabilities. The Soviets want to have *every* capability that technology can give them, in order to provide maximum options and flexibility.

The capability to launch a "frustrating" nuclear attack is also the capability to attack at leisure or to *threaten* attack in order to accomplish Soviet political objectives.

3. The changed military balance will weaken free world alliance systems and increase Soviet aggressiveness.

The cohesion of the free world since the emergence of the Soviet, and later the Chinese, threat has depended upon the conviction of our allies that the United States would always be willing to defend them in a military crisis. This conviction in turn has rested on the belief that the level of U.S. superiority over the Soviet Union was such that the Soviet Union would be deterred from launching an attack in the first place. Even the Soviet achievement of "parity" with the United States in the strategic forces tends to cast grave doubt on the assumption, and the establishment of a clear-cut Soviet strategic military superiority might well shatter it completely. Appreciating this, the Soviet leaders are likely to become emboldened to undertake a campaign of threats and intimidation on a far greater scale than they have so far employed. At best, our allies might succumb to these pressures through political accommodations on Soviet terms. At worst, the Soviets might launch actual invasions—against West Germany, for example, or in support of the Arabs against Israel, thus confronting U.S. leaders with major crises in which they would no longer enjoy the kind of credible military position advantage which has caused the Soviet Union to back down on previous occasions. As Zbigniew Brzezinski, a former foreign policy advisor to President Johnson, recently pointed out,

> "Greater capacity to become involved in the world's trouble spots will, in all probability, stimulate greater temptations to become so involved . . . As Soviet long-range air and sea-lift capabilities grow, the probabilities of a new type of confrontation—a direct one between U.S. and Soviet intervention forces—will similarly grow." [18]

In the same article, Mr. Brzezinski pointed out that until now peace has been safeguarded by a deterrence based on our considerable nuclear superiority. But now this superiority no longer exists and if present trends are not reversed, our enemies will soon enjoy the clear-cut superiority we once held.

In earlier phases of the cold war, the Soviets never believed that they enjoyed strategic superiority. Awareness of their military deficiencies and U.S. strength inhibited them in many situations, notably in the Cuban crisis. We cannot count on similar restraint today.

The urgency of the Safeguard Missile Defense System.

In view of these conclusions we believe that President Nixon was entirely correct when he said during his campaign for the Presidency:

> "At this time I do not believe that the United States can afford to accept the concept of parity with the Soviet Union. I believe that we face a potentially dangerous situation . . . to negotiate a de-escalation of trouble points around the world, whether in the Mideast or Viet Nam or Western Europe or what have you, if the next President of the United States goes into those conferences with the possibility that the Soviet Union rather than the United States is in a stronger power position, I think that we would not be able to effectively reach the goals that we want to reach . . . And at any kind of negotiation when one side wants to expand and the other side wants to defend, make sure

---

18. *Encounter*, November 1968.

that the side in that negotiation which is in the defensive position has more strength than the other side. That is why I would restore the strength of the United States, keep it at a proper level at this point, so that we would not be afraid to negotiate."

Nixon on the Issues, p. 15.

In the present situation, we believe that there cannot be any substitute for the maintenance of U.S. strategic military superiority. This superiority must be substantial because U.S. policies have always permitted the enemy the first blow. In a nuclear war, an enemy might wipe out a very large percentage of our weaponry (and population) in a first strike. Unless we have enough military strength to survive a first strike and still strike back decisively, the risk of a nuclear war increases.

Avoidance of war *requires* that the United States maintain overall military superiority, rather than acceptance of any kind of "parity" which can only be ephemeral and inherently unstable.

For more than two decades, the heart and core of America's strategy has been deterrence of Soviet aggression. This deterrence has been accomplished by establishing and maintaining a nuclear retaliatory strike force that could survive a surprise attack and still retain the capacity to inflict unacceptable damage on the Soviet Union.

If the United States is to continue as a viable and independent society, we should as a first step, create a missile defense system to protect our nuclear deterrent. Such a system will not, by itself, restore the military superiority which we have now lost. This essential first step is necessary if we are to reverse the sharp shift now taking place in the world's power balance.

Protecting our retaliatory missiles is important because the United States has no intent of striking the first blow in a global conflict.

Thus the refusal of the United States to consider a first strike makes it all the more important that the retaliatory force be protected against a Soviet attack. And it is to this end that a Safeguard anti-ballistic missile system has been recommended by the President of the United States.

In addition, the Safeguard system is designed (as was the earlier Sentinel concept) to afford defense (of heavily populated areas) against the type of attack Communist China is likely to be able to mount sometime in the 1970s.

The underlying logic of the ABM concept is that an enemy is unlikely to launch a nuclear attack on the United States, or credibly threaten such an attack if he knows that U.S. retaliatory forces will survive—forces that would result in his own destruction.

The opposition to Safeguard.

Opponents of Safeguard generally base their arguments on one or more of the following grounds:

1. It Wont Work.

The "Won't Work" argument is seriously flawed on both specific and general grounds. Both the Spartan and Sprint missiles—the prime ingredients of the proposed Safeguard system—already have been successfully flown. These in turn are successors to the Nike series of missiles which were successfully employed to knock down other missiles. The prototype missile radar is in test operation at the present time. The initial deployment of the Safeguard missile defense is now necessary to give us further technical, engineering, production and testing experience to improve the system. We learn by doing.

Safeguard will "work" in the sense it is intended to work. It is a "point" defense. A point defense is easier to achieve than an area defense since the enemy warhead can be usefully engaged at much closer proximity to its target. This in turn increases the time allowed the defense to track and react and greatly facilitates the separating out of decoys from the live warheads. Some people may feel that since *all* missiles may not be destroyed, the system is a failure. They say, "You may knock down nine, but the tenth will get through." But even if this is so, the enemy is forced to greatly multiply his arsenal with greatly sophisticated missiles before he could dare to attack. This enormously complicates his offensive problem and adds immeasurably to the deterrent effectiveness of our own offensive missiles.

In a larger sense, however, the United States has amply demonstrated its capacity to produce and operate the most complex communications, electronic and nuclear warfare systems. It is well to remember that some people declared the hydrogen bomb was impossible or that ICBMs and Polaris missile systems would not work. Moreover, the astonishing technical capacity revealed in the Apollo moon program or the Telestar communications satellites is evidence of what the United States can accomplish.

Throughout the history of warfare, every offense has produced a corresponding defense. To argue that no defense can ever be possible against missiles is to fly in the face of historical precedent. And it is to fly in the face of the opposite conclusions reached by the Soviet

66

Union. It is doubtful that the Soviets would have devoted the resources they have to ABM if they had concluded that it "Won't Work."

2. Safeguard is "too costly."

There are two broad sub-categories of this argument. One is the technical one relating to the relative costs of defensive systems and the corresponding offensive weapons needed to penetrate them. The other is that the nation cannot "afford" missile defense because of the overriding priority of domestic, social and economic programs.

On the first point, there are indications that the relative cost-ratios of offense/defense may be approaching parity. For example, D. G. Brennan, former President of the Hudson Institute made this recent observation:

> "Several years ago, it was widely believed that missile defenses were easy to penetrate—so easy that offensive increments costing only one or a few percent of the cost of opposing defense would serve to nullify it. In recent years, however, it has become apparent that cheap forms of decoys and other penetration aids cannot be relied upon to nullify modern defense techniques. A good defense can be overcome, but it is difficult. This is reflected in the fact that cost exchange ratios for a good defense are now believed to be in the region of one to one—perhaps one-third or two, but not one-tenth or ten. Thus, it is about as expensive to nullify a good defense as to build it." [19]

Even if we accept an estimate that missile defense may be two or three times more expensive than the offsetting attack, appropriate limited deployment could still force the attacker into greater expenditures than have been spent on defense. It is, therefore, of the utmost importance to find out whether effective defense can indeed be established for an expenditure which we can afford. This question cannot be answered by research alone. A limited deployment which may also be considered as a pilot operation is needed.

In weighing the second aspect of the cost question—the matter of national priorities—the American people would do well to consider the ultimate worth of the system, which is measured in the safety of millions and the survival of the nation. Without survival there will be no ghetto to rehabilitate. If we surrender as an independent nation to Soviet nuclear blackmail, it will be Soviet "welfare" programs we will live under and not our own.

Dr. Brennan threw further light on the cost factor when he wrote in an earlier article:

19. "The Case For Missile Defense," *Foreign Affairs*, April 1969, p. 435.

"The cost of ABM is not out of line when one considers what this country has spent over the last 18 years trying to put up some kind of air defense against Soviet bombers. In terms of 1968 dollars, the United States investment for the air defense system alone is probably on the order of $50 billion . . . Today we're talking about spending half that much on the investment cost in missile defense . . . (Dr. Brennan wrote this in relation to the cost of the original Sentinel ABM) . . . As it is, I would say that the $50 billion spent on air defense purchased an awful lot less insurance for our country than it is likely to obtain in the near future with a missile defense system." [20]

Certainly, foes of the Safeguard ABM system do no service to the nation when they underestimate the economic capacity of the United States. This capacity is far greater than many people realize. The Soviets have an advantage in the apparent lack of self-confidence among Americans in their own capacity to meet all of the nation's needs.

3. ABM is unnecessary: Deterrence is assured because U.S. retailatory power will always be sufficient to destroy the Soviet Union if she attacks us.

The Soviets are serious people and they have long since rejected the hypothesis that the offense alone guarantees deterrence. Their military policy is to create a balance of offensive and defensive power. How each will develop in relation to the other over future years is impossible to judge, they say. We think they make sense. If we counter Soviet ABM progress only by increasing our own offensive missiles we would be gambling on the assumption that defense technology will not eventually overcome offensive weapons systems.

Furthermore, the more the number and diversity of offensive and defensive systems the U.S. has in being at any time the more difficult it is for an aggressor to assess the probable effectiveness of a first strike and hence the more effective our deterrent becomes.

4. Development of a U.S. ABM will only stimulate the arms race.

Will the Soviets now cease any further augmentation of their offensive striking power if the United States unilaterally refrains from missile defense? Will they cease their own ABM efforts? The burden of proof for such contentions falls heavily on its advocates. We know that the Soviets have not ceased offensive missile production, because they have drawn past the United States; they are still building at a rapid rate. And we know from their statements that the Soviet leader-

---

20. "ABM: Yes or No?" Center for the Study of Democratic Institutions paper 1969.

ship holds that active defense constitutes a vital component of the nation's military capabilities. It seems only reasonable to conclude that the Soviet leaders would regard U.S. failure to develop an ABM as a sign of deficient military thinking—one that should be exploited, not followed.

5. **There should be a moratorium on U.S. ABM deployment while we try negotiations with the U.S.S.R.**

The difficulty with this argument is that it concedes to our adversaries the precious commodity of time. We are probably ahead of the Soviets in the level of our anti-missile technology, but how long can we expect this to continue, since Soviet military research and development expenditures are running at a greater rate than ours.

It is unlikely that a U.S. ABM moratorium would be followed by the Soviet Union because a) the Soviets are committed doctrinally to ABM no matter what the United States does and b) there is the complicating factor of Communist China. There are some indicators that the Soviet ABM system is being deployed partially against the potential Chinese threat to the U.S.S.R. If this is so, we cannot in any case expect the Soviets to dismantle or halt their ABM deployment because of any possible agreement with the United States. But if they continue to deploy and perfect their system—even if we were to concede that it was directed *entirely* against Red China (which is not the case)—the Soviets would be in possession of a weapons system which could just as easily be used to neutralize U.S. retaliatory missile forces.

6. **Safeguard would be "provocative" to the U.S.S.R. It would "damage the cause of peace."**

This argument rests on the thesis that the restoration of nuclear symmetry, through a U.S. ABM to match that of the Soviets, would be more destabilizing than the present asymmetrical situation which is developing between a balanced offensive-defensive U.S.S.R. force and an offensive-only U.S. posture. To the extent that Safeguard is designed primarily as a defense of our retaliatory forces and not of our people it cannot be construed as indicative of a U.S. intention to attack them. The "provocative" argument also neglects the fact that the Soviets have deployed their ABM around cities (thus supporting a possible first strike intention) without worrying that this might be "provocative" to the United States.

7. **Safeguard would lead to the domination of U.S. society by the "military-industrial complex."**

In this regard a basic truth must be kept in mind: unless the United States people wish to concede the world struggle to Communism by default, U.S. armed forces, and the industrial establishment to support them, are and will be necessary. Unless the officers of these armed forces provide the nation with their best professional judgment on what is needed to counter the military threat of our potential enemies, they will not be doing the job they are paid to do.

In the United States military judgment is subject to civilian review, as it should be. No military professionals in any country can boast a better record for honoring this principle than is the case in the United States. Fears of military "domination" or "take over" in the United States have no factual basis and run completely counter to every tradition of our society.

In the case of Safeguard our best military judgment has been reviewed and accepted by our highest civilian leadership. We are convinced that the American people can rely on that judgment.

Conclusions

Our President has asked for Safeguard. He wishes to enter into negotiations with the Soviet Union. He feels that he needs the system in order to bargain effectively with the Soviet Union, at least from a position of equality. If the nation refuses him this request it will seriously undercut his hand by repudiating him on an issue which he considers vital to the conduct of foreign relations.

On balance, Safeguard makes sense:

> . . it makes sense to defend our retaliatory missile sites;
>
> . . it makes sense to defend our air bases;
>
> . . it makes sense to defend our national command centers in the nation's capital;
>
> . . it makes sense because the cost is relatively low and the program is subject to yearly review;
>
> . . it makes sense to defend against the Chinese threat of the mid-70s;
>
> . . it makes sense because we are not foreclosing the future.

We are leaving our options open.

Anti-ballistic missile defense is not a cure-all for the security of the United States. It is not the ultimate defense system, for technology knows no limits and each decade produces fresh challenges and fresh need for response on the part of free nations. But anti-missile defense is an essential component in the network of military systems designed to give the American people a seamless garment of security in an age of acute danger.

Safeguard Makes Sense for Moral Reasons

ABM is a method of deterrence which will save lives and not destroy them. An effective ABM in the hands of *both* sides would at least lower the level of fatalities on both sides.

The Soviet Union recognizes the value of preserving the lives of its citizens. Ironically, the United States has placed emphasis upon retaliation, while the Soviets are actively deploying an ABM system supplemented by a comprehensive civil defense program to protect their population.

It is more consistent with the moral objectives of the United States for this country to provide more effective ways of protecting people than to base our deterrent power wholly upon our ability to kill people in other countries or "accept" heavy casualties at home.

We firmly believe that an American ABM system is the soundest insurance for peace and against war that the United States can buy in 1969, for the 1970's. Far from being an offensive weapon, the ABM is in reality insurance against war. It may well be, in fact, the single most important step the United States can take toward a real and lasting peace at this moment in history.

—In an article which included discussion of the ASC study in THE BALTIMORE SUNDAY SUN, Dudley Digges says:

". . . the ABM question . . . is being argued at the highest level of competence and responsibility, with—so far— generally honest, rather than politically self-serving conviction."

". . . issues such as those covered in this study are so vital that Americans must lay aside domestic political differences and work together in deciding what must be done in the interest of national security. This is why we have always sought the best Republican and Democrat, liberal, moderate and conservative thinking on how to meet national security problems. We selected the members of this committee on the basis of their **qualifications** rather than their **political** leanings."

—**John M. Fisher, President, American Security Council**

". . . we're not nuclear experts. But we prefer the ABM views of such nuclear and military experts as Libby, Thaler and Twining, to those of habitual disarm fans."

—**NEW YORK DAILY NEWS**

". . . a truly compelling ABM study."

—**Wm. R. Hearst, Jr., Editor-in-Chief, The Hearst Newspapers**

". . . the ASC report, is to the effect that the President needs Safeguard in order to bargain effectively with the Russians . . . most Americans will be unable to make heads or tails of the scientific argument. But when the chips are down it is very unlikely that they will want to repudiate the President on something that he says is needed both in his conduct of foreign affairs and in safeguarding the country."

—**WASHINGTON STAR**